The
Business Traveller's
Handbook

Turkey
The Business Traveller's Handbook

published by
Gorilla Guides
128 Kensington Church Street
London W8 4BH
Tel: 44 20 7221 7166 Fax: 44 20 7792 9288
E-mail: stacey.international@virgin.net

ISBN: 1 903185 01 7

Series Editor: Max Scott
Editor (Turkey): Hugh Davis
Production: Kitty Carruthers & Sam Crooks
Design: Nimbus Design
Printing & Binding: Tien Wah Press, Singapore

CIP Data: A catalogue record for this book is available from the British Library

Picture Credits:- *Cover (l)* Stuart Turpin (ffotograff); *Cover (r)* Nick Tapsell (ffotograff); *Half-title (tl)* Nick Tapsell (ffotograff), *(tr)* Michael Barron, *(bl)* Sheila Paine, (ffotograff), *(br)* Paul Greening (ffotograff); *Title page*: Jose Navarro (ffotograff); *page 4*, Michael Barron; *page 6 (t)* Stuart Turpin (ffotograff), *(b)* Jose Navarro (ffotograff), *(m)* Michael Barron; *page 7 (t)* James Nash, (ffotograff), *(b)* Nick Tapsell (ffotograff).

Turkey

The Business Traveller's Handbook

A typical street scene in Trabzon.

▲ The Blue Mosque in İstanbul.

▶ Blue tiles are typical decorative features in Islamic architecture.

▼ Lycian tombs in the ruins of the old city of Myra, Demre.

▲ Kiz Kalesi (Maiden Castle), Corycos.

▼ Making pita bread in Taksim, İstanbul.

CONTENTS

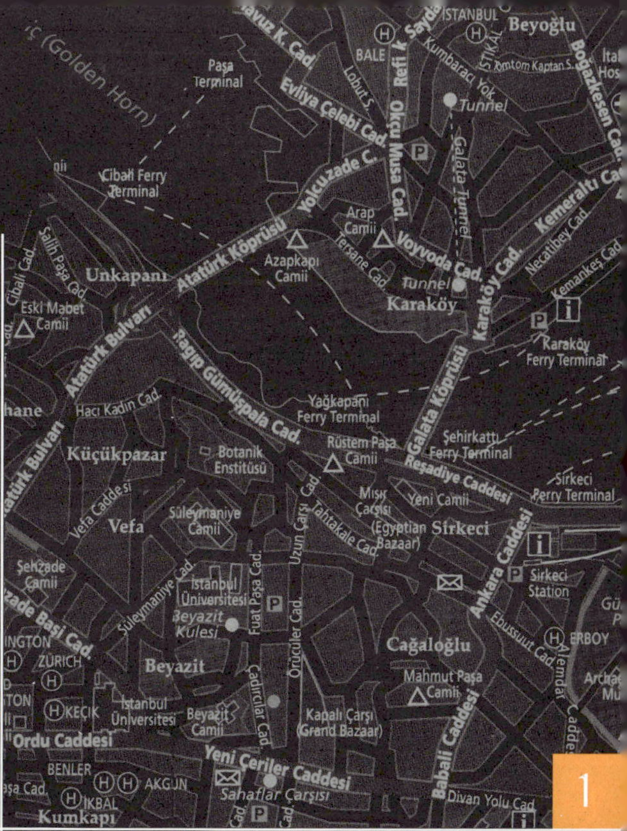

1

Turkey yesterday and today

1

Turkey yesterday and today

History

The area now occupied by Turkey and the Turkic peoples themselves both have long histories but the two did not come together until the eleventh century AD. Before that, the Anatolian peninsula and the European part of modern-day Turkey were occupied by a series of different peoples and had seen several empires come and go.

Ancient Turkey

Turkey was one of the earliest parts of the Mediterranean basin to be settled. The Stone Age 'city' of Çatal Höyük (south-east of Konya) had developed by 7500 BC. By the Bronze Age, the flourishing city-based civilisation of the Hatti or proto-Hittites had emerged, laying the foundations for the first Anatolian empire of the Hittites. This empire lasted from 1900 BC to around 1200 BC before being extinguished at approximately the same time as the Greek attack on the city of Troy in north-west Anatolia. Much is known about Hittite culture from the large amount of pottery and metalwork that they left behind in the area.

While the Greeks occupied the Aegean seaboard, the Anatolian interior fractured into a number of smaller kingdoms which were easily defeated by the Persian emperor Cyrus (529 BC) as he swept through the peninsula to the Aegean coast to harass the Greeks. At the opposite end of the peninsula, Alexander the Great conquered all before him in 334 BC on his expedition eastwards. After Alexander's death and the division of his empire, Anatolia again splintered into small states. These states were progressively absorbed into the expanding Roman empire between 190 BC and 47 BC. The kingdom of Pergamum was bequeathed to Rome in 133 BC and became the province of 'Asia' with its capital at Ephesus. The province played a key role in the early history of Christianity and there are many sites in Turkey with strong Biblical connections. Indeed the term Christian is reputed to have been coined at Antioch (now Antakya), a city which also lays claim to the first cathedral. The final residence of the Virgin Mary has been placed near Ephesus and the town of Tarsus (birthplace of St Paul) is in southern Turkey.

Early Christianity

In AD 305 the Roman emperor Diocletian abdicated. A lengthy and confused civil war followed until Constantine

Constantine

emerged as sole emperor in 324. Six years later he inaugurated his new capital on the site of the old Greek settlement of Byzantium on the European shore of the Bosphorus, the narrow stretch of water that divides the Anatolian peninsula from Europe and links the Black Sea with the Sea of Marmara.The new city was named Constantinople after its founder (İstanbul is the Turkicised version of this name) and flourished even as the western Roman Empire disintegrated. The eastern empire reached its peak under Justinian (527-65 AD) who consolidated Anatolia, the Balkans, Egypt and Syria, and even reconquered Italy and North Africa. He also ordered the building of a new church, to be the centre of Christianity. The result was the Aya Sofya. After Justinian's death, the Byzantine Empire began a long slow decline assailed by Slavs in the Balkans, Persians from the east and, starting in the late seventh century, Muslim Arabs from the south.

Byzantine territory was also periodically overrun by the migrating tribes from the Central Asian steppes. These nomads were expert horsemen with a strong martial tradition. The existence of Turkic peoples was first recorded by Chinese chroniclers in the fourth century AD. The term Turk is thought to derive from the name *Tu-Kue* given to these peoples by the Chinese. In recognition of their military value, Turkic troops were incorporated into the armies of the Islamic Arab empires where they often came to exercise effective control of the state. The first Turkish empire was founded in the early eleventh century, in what is now Iran, by the Seljuk dynasty but their prowess soon led to the conquest of much of Anatolia as well as present day Iraq. A remnant of the Seljuk empire survived in Anatolia until it was overrun, like much else, by the Mongol horde in 1243.

The Mongols

The Mongol pressure had prompted further western migration by Turkic peoples. Anatolia was a patchwork of small Turkic states continually harassing the Byzantines in a series of raids. One of the most successful raiders was a Turk named Ertuğrul whose son Osman was able to take advantage of the weakness of the Byzantines and the eclipse of the Seljuks to take over much of Anatolia. The resulting dynasty was named after Osman: the Turkish term Osmanlı ultimately became the English 'Ottoman'. The Ottomans expanded their empire by conquest and in 1453, the Ottoman Sultan Mehmet

The Ottomans

completed the extinction of the eastern Roman empire with the capture of Constantinople. The city was proclaimed the new Ottoman capital and a massive building programme undertaken. The Aya Sofya and many other churches were converted into mosques.

The Ottoman empire reached its height in the mid-sixteenth century under Sultan Süleyman the Magnificent, known to the Turks as 'the Lawgiver'. During this period the empire included much of the Balkans, Syria and Egypt. After Süleyman, the empire began its slow decline to become the 'Sick Man of Europe' in the nineteenth century and the subject of Western European political intrigues. Under pressure from the Russian and Austro-Hungarian empires, Turkey lost most of its Balkan territories but Anatolia remained to become the heartland of the modern republic of Turkey.

Modern Turkey

The modern history and politics of Turkey begins with the collapse of the Ottoman empire at the end of the First World War. Attempts by British, French, Greek and Italian forces to occupy İstanbul and parts of the Anatolian peninsula were resisted by remnants of the Ottoman army gathered together and inspired by Mustafa Kemal who had previously gained fame and popularity commanding the Turkish resistance to the allied invasion of the Gallipoli peninsula during the war. Mustafa Kemal was a charismatic figure who reinvigorated the demoralised Ottoman troops with the vision of a strong Turkish state, freed of the burden of empire.

Attatürk

Having seen off the allied invasions and established Turkey's right to exist as an independent state, Mustafa Kemal set about putting his vision into practice. He abolished the sultanate, sent the last sultan into exile and moved the capital to Ankara. Traditional dress including the fez for men and the woman's veil was outlawed as anachronistic and symbolic of Ottoman oppression. Mustafa Kemal's vision was of a modern, democratic and Western-oriented state. All adults were given the vote and a parliament elected. Mustafa Kemal was voted in as first president of the new Republic. He abolished the use of the Arabic script for writing Turkish and introduced an adapted version of the Latin alphabet. Introducing the concept of family names he took the surname Atatürk ('father of the Turks') and henceforth was known as Kemal Atatürk.

Kemal Atatürk

Atatürk's legacy was a modern and self confident state but one that was highly centralised and authoritarian. The military were seen as guardians of this new secular society, and it is a role they continue to take very seriously. Atatürk's charisma and his massive contribution to establishing the modern Turkish state led to the creation of a strong personality cult. Although Atatürk died in 1938, his image and personality continue to be an important part of Turkish politics. The Republican People's Party that Atatürk founded remained the only legal political party until reforms were implemented after the Second World War. Turkey remained neutral during most of the war but declared war on Germany in the last days of the conflict in order to be eligible for US reconstruction aid. After the war, Turkey was a founding member of the UN.

WWII

Post war Turkey has been beset by internal conflict and military *coups*. The armed forces led coups and intervened in 1960, '70 and '80 because of dissatisfaction with the conduct of politicians and a perception that they had exceeded their powers. A series of violent clashes between extreme right and left wingers in the late 1970s prompted the 1980 *coup*. The year 1990 was approached with understandable nervousness but there was no fourth direct military intervention. The armed forces had returned the country to civilian rule in 1983 under Turgat Ozal who implemented wide ranging economic and political reforms, inspired by the British prime minister, Margaret Thatcher. However, the greater sense of freedom, a growing sense of economic frustration and increasing disenchantment with mainstream politicians led to the emergence of a popular Islamist political party. The Refah won the largest share of the vote in the 1995 general election but was kept out of power by military-inspired manoeuvrings by the other political powers. Eventually, in 1996, The Refah was allowed to participate in a coalition government. The military persisted with their campaign to exclude Refah and the party was banned in 1997 under the pretext that it was endangering the country's secular constitution.

Islamic Movement

The 1980s also saw the emergence of Kurdish separatism. The Marxist Kurdistan Workers' Party (PKK) launched an insurgency against Turkish forces in the Kurdish heartland of south-east Turkey. The conflict led to thousands of deaths on both sides and accusations from Kurdish groups,

Turkish organisations and international observers of severe abuses of human rights on both sides. By 1998, Turkish forces had all but defeated the Kurds and PKK leader Abdullah Ocalan was captured in February 1999. However, the conflict has left a legacy of mistrust on both sides by its duration and brutality. The PKK staged terrorist attacks in Turkish tourist resorts and kidnapped foreigners who strayed into the south-east region. Turkish forces also used harsh tactics against those suspected of supporting the insurgency. The threat from the PKK is greatly reduced but has not totally disappeared.

DYP

President Süleyman Demirel is a centre-right politician who first became Prime Minister in 1965 but was removed in 1971 following the military coup of the previous year. He was unable to return to politics until the late 1980s, when he became leader of the True Path Party (DYP) and won the largest share of the vote. Demirel was appointed prime minister for a second time by President Turgat Özal and was elected president in 1993 following Özal's sudden death from a heart attack. When his constitutional term of seven years was completed in May 2000, his place was taken by Ahmet Necdet Sezer (*see page 21*). Prime Minister Bülent Ecevit is a centre left politician who has also had a long and eventful career. He first served as Prime Minister in the early 1970s after the restoration of civilian rule following the 1970 *coup*. Like Demirel, he was subsequently excluded from political participation but continued to play a role behind the scenes and returned to public life in the mid 1990s as leader of the Democratic Left party (DSP). Demirel appointed him caretaker Prime Minister in the run up to the April 1999 general election. The DSP gained the largest share of the vote and Ecevit now heads a coalition government with the nationalist MHP.

DSP

Anap

Mesut Yilmaz is the long serving leader of the Motherland Party (Anap), which was founded by Turgat Özal. Demirel appointed Yılmaz Prime Minister in 1997 after the removal of Refah from office but he was unable to keep the coalition together and was forced to step down. The deep animosity between Yılmaz and the leader of the DYP, Tansu Çiller, has prevented the merger of the two parties. They did work together in a brief Çiller-led coalition government in 1996 but mutual hostility has prevented the formation of a strong centre-right force in Turkish politics.

Tansu Çiller

Tansu Çiller is leader of the centre-right True Path Party (DYP) and in 1993 became the country's first woman Prime Minister. Before entering politics, she was a professor of economics and this expertise led Demirel to appoint her to continue the country's economic reforms. Although Çiller made some progress by privatising state enterprises, she failed to put forward a coherent economic plan and the result was severe economic problems in 1994-5 resulting in a vote of no confidence. Her husband's business connections and allegations of links with organised crime have further undermined her credibility and popularity. This has directly affected the DYP's electoral standing but she has kept her post as party leader. There is little prospect of her returning to public office in the foreseeable future.

CHP

MHP

A number of other political parties also operate in present day Turkey. The CHP is the successor party to Atatürk's Republican People's Party but is not a major force in Turkish politics. Ecevit's DSP is one party that has emerged from splits within the CHP. Fazilet is the reincarnation of the banned Refah. Although it has attempted to differentiate itself from Refah in order to avoid the wrath of the military, it contains many ex-Refah members and will probably suffer the same fate. The MHP is a right-wing nationalist party and a junior coalition partner in the government after its better than expected performance in the April 1999 election. This performance was due to a surge in nationalist feeling following the capture of Abdullah Ocalan.The MHP has toned down its xenophobic rhetoric in recent years and attempted to distance itself from its violent past.

Turkey's role in the world

The Asia Minor peninsula and in particular the city of İstanbul have played a leading role in world affairs for several millennia. İstanbul was the centre of the Christian world for over a thousand years and then was the capital of the Ottoman empire – one of the world's major powers from 1453 to 1923. Since the end of the Ottoman era and the establishment of the Turkish Republic, Turkey has redefined its world role. The foundation of the republic involved ending the direct interference of outside powers in Turkish affairs with the expulsion of foreign occupying armies and the ending of special concessions to foreign residents. This has left a legacy of a strong feeling of independence and a reluctance to tolerate outside interference. In the first two decades of the Turkish republic, the government concentrated on building the new country and took a back seat in world affairs. During the Second World War, Turkey stayed neutral but declared war on Nazi Germany in the dying months in order to be eligible for aid under the Marshall Plan. However, since the Second World War, Turkey has adopted a more proactive foreign policy. The country was a founding member of the UN and NATO. It is also a member of several other key international and economic organisations including the OECD and the World Trade Organisation.

Europe and the European Union

A re-orientation of Turkey's international outlook towards Europe and away from the Middle East was an important factor in the development of the Turkish Republic. Since the 1960s, this has found expression in an ambition to join the EU. Successive governments, both civilian and military, have made membership an essential part of their foreign policy. Turkey views EU membership as bringing wide-ranging economic benefits and providing affirmation of its 'new' identity as a modern European nation. One of the major obstacles to Turkey becoming a candidate has been the EU's concern over Turkey's record of respect for human rights. In December 1999, Turkey achieved the most significant progress in its long-held ambition. At the EU Heads of Government summit in Helsinki, Finland Turkey was admitted to the list of candidate countries. However, Turkey is at the foot of a list of thirteen countries awaiting membership. Turkey's admission to the list does, though, mean that it can start the long negotiation process for membership.

This process could take up to ten years and will require considerable changes in Turkey's laws, regulatory systems and economy before it meets membership requirements. Although, EU membership is a widely accepted policy in Turkey and in the run-up to the EU's December 1999 decision there was little opposition to the prospect of membership, this is likely to change over the course of the negotiation process. The need to comply with EU membership requirements will call for radical changes in some areas. The transfer of power to Brussels over some policy areas is likely to conflict with Turkey's strong sense of national pride and intolerance of interference in its internal affairs. On the other hand, many Turks are likely to welcome EU efforts to strengthen regulation in some areas. The severity of the earthquake in August 1999 was blamed partly on lax adherence to building regulations. The process of converging with the EU has already started. Since 1st January 1996, Turkey has enjoyed a customs union with the EU. This has led to the dismantling of tariff barriers between Turkey and the EU. A wide range of Turkish goods can now enter the EU without paying customs duties. This has added to Turkey's attraction as a base for manufacturers hoping to exploit markets in the EU.

GNP Growth – Comparisons

In absolute terms, Turkey's Gross National Product is larger than Argentina and more than twice that of Greece or Portugal.

Russia, Caucasus and Central Asia

The collapse of the Soviet Union provoked a major re-evaluation of Turkey's foreign policy towards its Black Sea neighbours and countries further east. During the Cold War, Turkey was a frontline state in the confrontation between NATO and the Eastern bloc. Turkey was the only NATO state with a land border with the Soviet Union. The Soviet Union's collapse created the opportunity for Turkey to re-establish relations with ethnic Turks in the Caucasus and Central Asia. Turkey was determined to become the main trade gateway for these emerging markets and to benefit from exploitation of the region's huge hydrocarbon resources. Turkey and its allies, particularly the US, were keen to limit Iran's influence in the region. To an extent, Turkey has succeeded in gaining this role. Turkey played a leading role in establishing the Black Sea Economic Co-operation Organisation, which links Turkey with its Black Sea neighbours. Turkish Airlines has also established regular airlinks with destinations in the

Caucasus and Central Asia, making İstanbul an important transit point for business executives heading further east. The Turkish port of Ceyhan has long been the preferred choice as the terminus for the much-discussed plans for an oil export pipeline for Caucasian and Central Asian oil. (For more on this see Industry Overview: Oil, p 65).

Before he stepped down from power in May 2000 at the end of his presidential term, former President Süleyman Demirel had played a leading role in forging links with Turkic states in the former Soviet Union. First as Prime Minister and then as President, Demirel articulated a vision of pan-Turkism that built on the country's shared linguistic heritage to develop strong business and economic links. This was largely a personal vision and the President's traditional strong role in foreign policy gave Demirel the scope to pursue it. Over the course of his career this vision was only reluctantly shared by successive governments who have wanted to concentrate on relations with the EU. Demirel's retirement and his replacement by a non-politician as president is likely to lead to a reduction in the emphasis placed on relations with the former Soviet Union's Turkic states. Demirel's replacement, Ahmet Necdet Sezer, is a judge, has little political experience and lacks a strong interest in foreign affairs. Remarks early in his term of office suggested that he shared the government's desire to press ahead with EU membership as the main thrust of foreign policy.

NATO

The US

The US State Department describes its relations with Turkey as 'complex and multi-faceted'. The complexity stems from Turkey's role as a significant military ally on the one hand and the weakness of some of its civil institutions along with its involvement in long-running disputes on the other. As already noted, Turkey played a key role in NATO during the Cold War and has remained a stalwart of the organisation following the end of the conflict. Turkey is still an important base for US troops and the US maintains an airbase at İncirlik (south-eastern Turkey) from where it enforces the no-fly zone against Iraq. Turkey contributed forces to the allied effort to expel Iraq from Kuwait in 1991 and also played a high profile role in the NATO expulsion of Serbian forces from Kosovo in 1999. Turkey is therefore an important ally both in south-eastern Europe and the Middle East.

Greece

Turkey's long-running antagonism towards Greece and its continued occupation of northern Cyprus (see below, the Cyprus Question) strain the overall good relations with the US. Traditionally poor relations between Turkey and Greece (which is also a NATO member and US ally) has long irritated the US as it limits co-operation in the region and hinders a solution to the Cyprus question. The US also remains concerned about Turkey's record of respect for human rights and the weakness of some of its democratic institutions. However, this is balanced by US concern over the rise of Islamism in the country. The US has in the past tolerated military coups and continued direct military involvement in Turkish politics due to the positive impact on the country's stability.

The Cyprus Question

Turkey's efforts to join the EU have long been thwarted by the EU's insistence on a solution to the division of Cyprus before Turkey could be admitted to the EU. The EU lifted that condition at the December 1999 Helsinki summit but will continue to apply pressure on Turkey to work towards a solution. In 1974, Turkey sent troops to Cyprus to defend the Turkish Cypriot community and established a Turkish Cypriot administration in the northern third of the island. This administration was declared the independent Turkish Republic of Northern Cyprus (TRNC) in 1983 but was recognised only by Turkey. The Greek-dominated Republic of Cyprus government based in southern Cyprus remains the internationally recognised government. The Northern Cypriot economy has not developed at the same pace as its southern counterpart and the areas remains economically underdeveloped. Agriculture and tourisn are the main economic activities and the Northern Cypriot government is supported by subsidies and grants from Ankara. The lack of international recognition for the TRNC complicates the business environment and adds to the risk of doing business there. The area has become something of an offshore haven for Turkey.

Northern Cyprus travel advice

Business executives should ensure that TRNC officials do not put entry and exit stamps in their passport but on a separate piece of paper. The Greek and Cypriot authorities will refuse entry to any one who has evidence of travel to the TRNC in their passport.

Turkish Airlines (THY) has regular flights to Lefkosia (known as Nikosia to most non-Turks) airport from İstanbul, Ankara, Adana and Antalya. İstanbul Airlines also flies to Lefkosia from İstanbul.

Ferry and hydrofoil services link Taşucu (near Silifke, west of Mersin) in Turkey with the northern Cypriot port of Girne.

Religion

Religion

Islam is the dominant religion in Turkey, with 99 per cent of the population being Muslim. Although the Turkish constitution strictly separates state and religion, Islam still plays an important role in Turkish society. Religious observance is strong, especially in rural and working class areas and partly accounts for the popularity of Islamist political parties in Turkey. Islam is part of Turkey's heritage and there is a great deal of pride in Turkey's history. The secular nature of Turkey means that religious observance and piety remain private matters and play little role in public life.

The Cyprus Problem

Turkey's 1974 occupation of northern Cyprus followed years of confrontation between the Greek and Turkish communities on the island. Turkish Cypriots had withdrawn from the carefully balanced power-sharing government in response to inter-communal violence and had formed their own municipal administrations prior to 1974. The precise provocation for the 1974 invasion was an attempted coup backed by the military government in Greece against the then Cypriot President Archbishop Markarios. Both Greece and Turkey had powers under the Cypriot constitution to intervene to defend their respective communities and in 1974, Turkey took advantage of these powers.

Size and Population

- Turkey is one of the largest countries in Europe in terms of area and in terms of population.
- After Russia, Turkey has the second largest European country in area and has the third largest population in Europe after Russia and Germany, with one of the fastest population growth rates in Europe.
- At the same time, population density is low and the population is very young. Turkey will not suffer as badly from an ageing population as much of Western Europe in coming decades
- Finally, the population is primarily located in urban regions. Currently 59 per cent of the population live in cities or towns, a trend that has increased steadily over the years. This factor reinforces Turkey's progression from an agrarian to an industrial-based society.

1

First Impressions

Turkey is increasingly integrated into the world economic system and has sophisticated facilities for business travellers. The Turkish business community is Western-oriented and is accustomed to international business practices. You will find Turks very welcoming and hospitable. There are few strange customs or sensitivities of which the first-time business visitor must be aware. Turkey's main cities have a familiar look with billboards advertising international brands and well-known shops and businesses. However, this also means that business visitors face the same irritations as in other business destinations including traffic congestion, crowded public transport and petty crime.

Nicosia/ Lefkosia

Nicosia is a divided city. A stretch of no-man's-land, monitored by the UN, divides the two sides. Non-Greeks can cross from the South for the day but have to return before five or six pm on the same day. From the North there is no issue to the South, and the shortest way to get from the North of Nicosia to the South is by aeroplane changing at Istanbul, then at Athens.

The business traveller should also be aware of other hazards. In recent years, Kurdish and leftist extremists have staged terrorist attacks in urban areas. However, such attacks were always rare and in 1998 and 1999 the threat declined markedly.

Islam and Turkey

Islam arose in Arabia in the seventh century AD from the same monotheistic tradition that produced Judaism and Christianity. Islam sees itself as continuing that tradition but correcting errors. Muslims respect the sacredness of the Bible and Torah, recognise the authority of the Biblical prophets and believe that Muhammad is the last of these prophets. The Quran is the word of God as revealed to the Prophet Muhammad. However, Muhammad is not accorded any divine status.

Islam has five basic tenets: understanding and believing that there is only one god and that Muhammad is His prophet; praying in the direction of Makkah daily at five appointed times; giving alms to the poor; keeping the fast during the month of Ramadan; making the pilgrimage to Makkah at least once in every Muslim's lifetime if physically possible.The Quran provides instruction and advice on how Muslims should conduct themselves. Precepts include dressing modestly, avoiding pork, alcohol and some other foods and refraining from gambling and usury. Muhammad's sayings have also given rise to Islamic customs and traditions, while varying interpretations of the Quran and Muhammad's way of life as well as political disagreements have led to many splits in Islam over the centuries and the emergence of differing branches and sects. The main division between Sunnis and Shias occurred early in Islamic history. Shias believe that Muhammad's nephew Ali (his nearest male relative) should have succeeded to the leadership of the Islamic community on Muhammad's death. Sunnis accept the succession that actually took place and became the majority with Islam. Turkish Muslims are overwhelmingly Sunni.

BULGARIA
GREECE
Black Sea
Bosphorus
N
0 75 150 kms
0 75 150 m
GEORGIA
AZER.
ARMENIA
IRAN
IRAQ
SYRIA
CYPRUS
Mediterranean Sea
Aegean Sea
G
R
E
E
C
E
İstanbul
Sea of Marmara
İzmit
Zonguldak
Samsun
Hopa
Trabazon
Bolu
Gemlik
Bursa
Çanakkale
Balikesir
Eskişehir
ANKARA
Sivas
Euphrates
Erzurum
Lake Van
Van
Manisa
İzmir
Kayseri
Pamukkale
Aydin
Konya
Kahramanmaras
Adıyaman
Diyarbakir
Tigris
Şanliurfa
Gaziantep
Adana
Antalaya
Mersin
İskenderun
Antakya

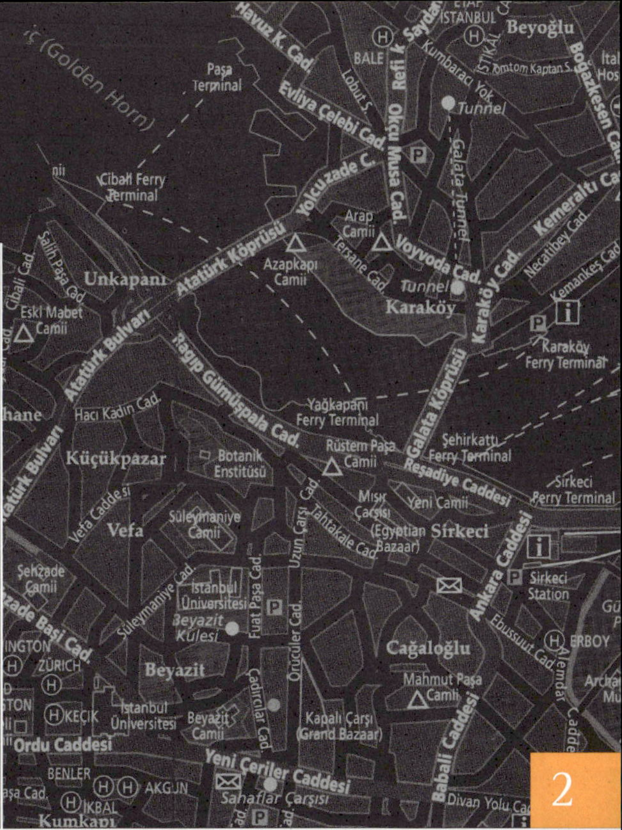

2

exploring the potential market

2

exploring the potential market

An outline of some of the myriad organisations which exist to assist the businessman or woman, along with an assessment of their focus and likely relevance.

Executives should be as well informed as possible before entering a market. This section acts as a guide to where to obtain the necessary information ahead of departure. It includes government and private sources in electronic and hardcopy format and discusses the availability of reliable market and economic information. Whether you are visiting Turkey for the first time or making the latest in a series of regular visits, preparation is essential to get the most out of the trip and ensure that your project succeeds. Obtaining the latest information will allow you to plan effectively for your trip, get a clear picture of the market you are entering and identify any trends or opportunities that you can use to your advantage and spot any possible pitfalls. It is equally important to ensure that the information you use is accurate and that you are aware of any possible bias.

The sources below provide a starting point for research on the Turkish market. Many of them are free or provide information at very little cost. Much of this information is not detailed enough for a thorough appraisal of the Turkish market and will only allow you to get an overview.

Turkish embassies

USA
2525 Massachusets. Ave. NW
Washington DC, 20008
❑ Tel: +1 202 612 6700; fax: +1 202 612 6744.
Website: [www.Turkey.org]

UK
43 Belgrave Square
London, SW1X 8PA
❑ Tel: +44 20 7393 0202; Fax: +44 20 7393 0066
Website: [www.turkishembassy-london.com].

Canada
197 Wurtemburg Street
Ottawa
Ontario, KIN 8L9
❑ Tel: +1 613 789 4044; fax: +1 613 789 3442.

Australia
60 Mugga Way, Red Hill
Canberra
ACT 2603
❑ Tel: +61 2 6295 0227; fax: +61 2 6239 6592.

US Ministries and other government agencies

The main United States source for information on overseas markets is the US Commercial Service, under the Department of Commerce's Trade Information Center. The US Commercial Service offers trade counselling and contacts, promotes US companies, researches markets, acts as an advocate to US businesses, provides information on financing, and checks the credit of possible overseas business partners, among other services.

Trade Information Center, International Trade Administration
US Department of Commerce, Washington DC 20230
❑ Tel: +1-800-USA-TRADE; Fax: 202-482-4473
E-mail: TIC@ita.doc.gov
Website: [www.ita.doc.gov]

This website contains a directory of trade contacts at the federal, state and local levels for US exporters. The directory can be viewed by state, division and zip code.

The State Department

The State Department and Department of Commerce provide a range of information to US companies or representatives of US companies operating in Turkey, including the *Country Commercial Guide*, an overview of the business climate in Turkey.

The *Country Commercial Guide* can be downloaded at [www.state.gov]

Contact details for the State Department's Turkey desk are:

Office of Southern Europe
Room 5511, US Department of State
2201 C Street NW
Washington, DC 20520
❑ Tel: +1 202 647 6114; Fax: +1 202 647 5087

Other useful sources are:

Turkey Desk
Office of Western Europe
US Department of Commerce
14th and Constitution Ave NW
Washington, DC 20005-4905
❑ Tel: +1 202 783 0483; Fax: +1 202 482 2897

American-Turkish Council
1010 Vermont Avenue NW
Suite 1020
Washington, DC 20005-4905
❑ Tel: +1 202 783 0483; Fax: +1 202 783 0511

Web Sites

Some of the best Turkey-related Web sites for executives are:

[www.turk-web.com], [www.turkindex.com], [www.searchturkiye.com], [www.asiaminor.com], [www.wec-net.com]

The US Department of Commerce oversees a number of Export Assistance Centers across the U.S. These are located in Appendix 1.

UK Ministries and other Government Agencies

2

Trade Partners UK

The primary British government source for information on overseas markets is Trade Partners UK. It produces a range of publications and offers other services including seminars and trade missions to small and medium sized companies wanting to break into new markets. It also provides practical help, advice and support for exporters, and gives access to the world wide network of overseas Commercial staff and locally engaged market experts.

Trade Partners UK operates an excellent library for exporters. It is free to use and you can find an extensive range of publications on Turkey and most other countries including directories, the latest Economist Intelligence Unit reports (see below) and country guides. Customers can now buy priced export publications on the Internet via the Export Publications website.

Export Market Information Centre
Kingsgate House
66-74 Victoria Street
London SW1E 6SW
❑ Tel: +44 207 215 5444/5; fax: +44 207 215 4231
E-mail: [EMIC@xpd3.bti.gov.uk]
Website: [www.brittrade.com/emic]

The Trade Partners UK exporter for Turkey can be contacted on ❑ Tel: +44 1706 810522.

The contact details for Trade Partners UK Turkey desk are:

Turkey Trade Unit
Room 417, Kingsgate House
66-74 Victoria Street
London SW1E 6SW
❑ Tel: +44 207 215 4914; fax: +44 207 215 4366

The Web

Turkey has taken to the Internet with enthusiasm and is one of the most Internet-literate countries in the region. There is, therefore, a multitude of Turkey-related websites claiming to give the best and latest information on the country. Some of the best for executives are: [www.turk-web.com], [www.turkindex.com], [www.searchturkiye.com], [www.asiaminor.com], [www.wec-net.com.]

Other sources

Chambers of Commerce or any trade or professional body that you belong to may be able to provide information on Turkey. They may not produce the material themselves but you will have access to their library where such data is held. These bodies may also offer the facility of conducting research on your behalf for a fee. This is a more costly method but is time-saving. You will have to be very specific in defining your research project to obtain the maximum benefit.

2

Turkish-British Chamber of Commerce and Industry
33 Bury Street
St James's
London SW1Y 6AX
❑ Tel: +44 20 7321 0999; fax: +44 20 7321 0989

Middle East Association
Bury House
33 Bury Street
London SW1Y 6AX
❑ Tel: +44 20 7839 2137; fax: +44 20 7839 6121

Digging Deeper

Once you have an overview of the market in Turkey, you may want more detailed economic information or wish to concentrate on your particular sector. This is where the cost of research starts to increase but you will be very well informed and the risk of unpleasant surprises later on will be much reduced. You will be aware of the trends and the possible effects on your business and therefore able to plan for them.

Economic and country guides

Dun & Bradstreet

The two best sources of detailed economic information and analysis are Dun & Bradstreet (D&B) and the Economist Intelligence Unit (EIU). D&B produce a Country Report on Turkey, which is available either in hardcopy or on CD-ROM and is updated every six months. It provides detailed analysis of the Turkish economy including political factors, short- and long-term issues and information on the trading and investing environments. D&B also produce two other publications helpful to exporters to Turkey. The first is the *Exporters' Encyclopaedia*, an annual publication that provides information and advice on exporting to almost every country in the world. The second is the *International Risk and Payment Review*, a monthly publication that allows companies to keep up to date on issues affecting the trading environment in Turkey.

D&B can be contacted at:

Austin
Texas 78731
❑ Tel: (800) 234 3867; or +1 512 794 7768
Website: [www.DNB.com]
To order online: custserv@dnb.com

Holmer's Farm Way
High Wycombe
Bucks, HP12 4UL
❑ Tel: +44 1494 422000; fax: +44 1494 422260
Website: [www.dunandbrad.co.uk].

Economist Intelligence Unit

The Economist Intelligence Unit produces a range of quarterly and annual publications which contain detailed political and economic analysis of Turkey. The most useful of these publications is the quarterly Country Forecast, which provides a detailed five-year outlook for Turkey. The EIU's Country Profile includes an annual overview of the country and Country Report provides a quarterly update on the market. Their on-line service Viewswire is a useful tool for monitoring developments in Turkey and other countries. The EIU also produces reports on the automotive, healthcare, telecommunications and financial sectors.

The EIU can be contacted at:
15 Regent Street
London SW1Y 4LR
❑ Tel: +44 20 7830 1000; fax: +44 20 7830 1023.
Website: [www.eiu.com].

Banks, particularly the larger institutions that operate across the globe, may also be a useful source of information. Barclays Bank produces a series of economic snapshots of most major world markets. These are available free from the bank's website, although quality can be questionable: [www.barclays.com].

Many of the companies and organisations mentioned above also provide information on specific sectors and industries in Turkey. The UK's Trade Partners UK produces reports on key sectors in Turkey and other markets, as does the EIU. Dun & Bradstreet is a reliable source of information on key companies.

Other companies providing market research in Turkey are:

International Business Services AS
Abdi İpekci Caddesi, Kızılkaya Apt 59/4
80200 Maçka
İstanbul
❑ Tel: +90 212 231 0481; fax: +90 212 231 6614.

Arthur Andersen & Co
Arjantin Caddesi, 17/6
06700 Kavaklıdere
Ankara
❑ Tel: +90 312 468 4081; fax: +90 312 468 4291.
Website: [www.arthurandersen.com].

Denet Touche Ross
Denet Mali Danişmanlik AS
Büyükdere Caddesi, 121
Ercan Han, Kat 4-6
80300 Gayrettepe
İstanbul
❑ Tel: +90 212 275 9690; fax: +90 212 272 3323
Website: [www.deloitte.com].

Travel Advice

Information about flights, visas and the like is contained in Chapter 3. This section deals with such matters as health concerns and security issues. The earthquakes in the north-west of the country in late 1999 demonstrate the need to obtain up to the minute advice on travel conditions.

The most convenient source of advice on travelling from the UK is the UK Foreign and Commonwealth Office (FCO) travel advisory service. This can be accessed free either by telephone or on-line. It provides succinct information and advice on natural disasters, health concerns, security and political issues. It is more than adequate for most business travellers' needs. Be aware though that it is aimed at a wide audience and is not geared solely towards the business visitor's requirements. The information may also be subject to political bias; negative comments on a country can have an adverse impact on the UK's relations with that country and therefore tend to be avoided.

FCO

The FCO travel advisory service can be contacted on:
❑ Tel: +44 20 7238 4503/4;
Website: [www.fco.gov.uk/travel], or on Ceefax on BBC2 page 470.

The US State Department advice service can be found at: [www.state.gov/travel_warnings]. These can sometimes seem alarmist as the US State Department is legally obliged to publish any threats to US citizens and their property of which it is aware.

For travel information and advice aimed specifically at the business traveller's needs, you should turn to the private sector. Here there are some good, but expensive, services which provide more frequently updated reports than the FCO or State Department travel notices. These services tend to be more forward looking, commenting for instance on the likelihood of further security incidents or the possible deterioration or improvement in the travel environment. They are also usually more frank about a country as they are not confined by the political restrictions under which the FCO or State Department must operate.

The main providers of these specialist services are: Control Risks, Kroll Associates and Pinkertons.

Control Risks offers two travel-related services: Business Traveller, a country-focussed service forming part of its

Specialist information services

Country Risk Forecast service and CityBrief [www.citybrief.com] which looks at individual cities. Both are online services available by subscription only.

Control Risks Group
83 Victoria Street
London SW1H 0HW
❑ Tel: +44 20 7222 1552; fax: +44 20 7222 2296
Website: [www.crg.com].

Kroll Associates produce a city-focussed service called Travel Watch and a service called Airline and Airport Watch with a more specific remit.

Kroll Associates
25 Savile Row
London W1X 0AL
❑ Tel: +44 20 7396 0000; fax: +44 20 7969 2631
Website: [www.krollworldwide.com].

Pinkertons offers a facility called Pinkerton's Global Intelligence Service which is updated daily and provides brief analysis on developments worldwide.

Pinkertons
205 Lower Richmond Road
Richmond, Surrey TW9 4LN
❑ Tel: +44 20 8392 6056; fax: +44 20 8382 2088
Website: [www.pinkertons.com].

Although you have thoroughly researched Turkey, your need for information, analysis and advice may not be over. You may require detailed information on prospective partners or analysis geared towards your specific project or the business environment that you are entering. Detailed investigation and analysis tailored to particular specifications are costly and really only viable for companies involved in large projects or where a lot is at stake. It is also advisable for companies considering a modest initial investment but with the intention of making a long-term commitment to Turkey.

The companies mentioned above – Control Risks, Kroll and Pinkertons – all provide tailor-made confidential assessments of the business environment in which you will operate in Turkey and provide detailed information on the people and companies with which you will form strategic partnerships.

Other companies that operate in this field are:

Deloitte & Touche Forensic Services
Hill House
1 Little New Street
London EC4A 3TR
❑ Tel: +44 207 936 3000; fax: +44 207 936 2638.
Website: [www.deloitte.co.uk].

Maxima Group plc
29 Queen's Anne Gate
London SW1H 9BU
❑ Tel: +44 207 227 3300; fax: +44 207 227 3311.
Website: [www.maximag.co.uk].

News and newspapers

To keep up to date with developments in your particular sector and in the wider market, the easiest method is to monitor the press and media for stories on Turkey. The country receives widespread coverage in the international press and most British newspapers and news organisations have correspondents based in the country. Internet editions of some newspapers and media organisations offer news e-mail services with stories on specified subjects sent to your e-mail address. Others allow you to produce customised pages, which are updated with stories on your chosen subjects. One of the best is CNN's service [www.cnn.com].

For a local perspective, the only English-language newspaper is the *Turkish Daily News* and its sister weekly publication *Probe*. Both are available on the Internet as well as in hardcopy by subscription. Website: [www.turkishdailynews.com].

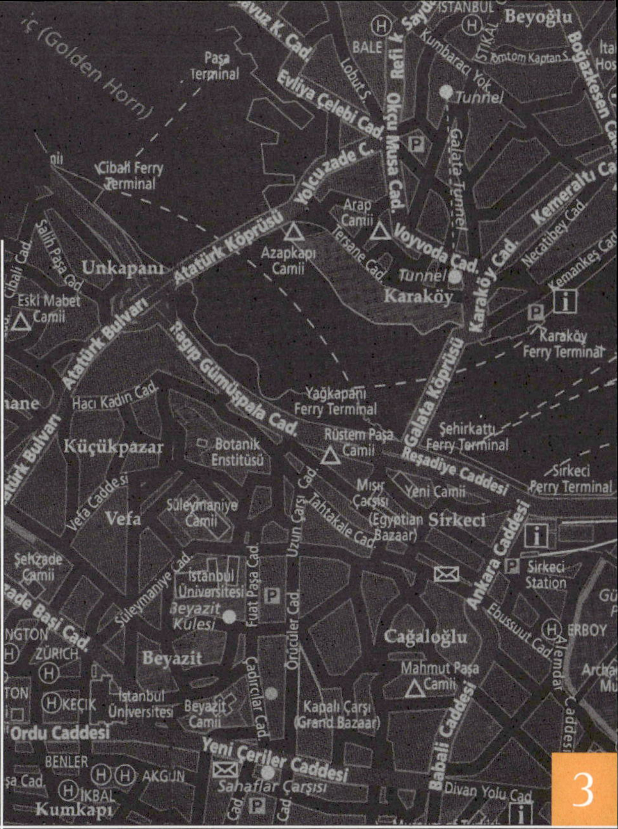

3

getting there

3

getting to Turkey

The various considerations in arranging travel to Turkey.

Turkey is keen to promote itself both as a business destination and as a hub for flights to the Caucasian and Central Asian republics of the former Soviet Union. Turkey is therefore well served by reputable airlines and the national carrier Turkish Airlines offers an efficient international and domestic service. Entry requirements are also fairly simple but do have one or two idiosyncrasies.

Entry Requirements

You should ensure that your passport is valid for at least three months beyond the end of your intended visit or you may be refused entry. Most Turkish visas are issued for three months and officials will only issue visas to passports valid for the entire period. Visas are usually issued at the point of entry to the country rather than at Turkish consulates overseas. Indeed, there are reports of border officials refusing to recognise visas issued at Turkish consulates. The following nationals require visas: British, Irish, US, Austrian, Israeli, Italian, Portuguese and Spanish. The following nationals do **not** require visas: Australian, Canadian, New Zealand, Belgian, Danish, Dutch, Finnish, French, German, Greek, Icelandic, Japanese, Norwegian, Swedish and Swiss.

Visas

British nationals are required to pay for their visa at the point of entry with a £10 note. This must be an English note; Scottish, Northern Irish and notes issued in the Channel Islands will be refused. No other currencies or form of payment including traveller's cheques will be accepted. US nationals must pay the $45 visa fee in cash (US dollars only) at the point of entry. In both cases, officials may refuse to accept badly damaged notes or those that have been defaced in any way.

By Air

The national airline, known by its Turkish initials THY, provides a reliable and comfortable service to a wide range of European and other cities. THY flies to both London Heathrow (three times daily) and Manchester (four times a week) in the UK and to New York, Chicago and Miami in the US. THY does not fly direct to Ireland, Australia, Canada or New Zealand. There are 15 daily flights between İstanbul and Ankara – a one-hour flight.
THY is a member of the Qualifyer airline alliance. This links it with Swissair, Austrian Airlines, Sabena, TAP Air

Airlines

Portugal, AOM French Airlines, Crossair, Lauda Air, Tyrolean Airways and Air Europe. Other Qualifyer partner airlines are AeroMexico, Air One, ANA-All Nippon Airways, Austrian Airtransport, Cathay Pacific Airways, Delta Air Lines, Finnair, Malaysia Airlines, Nationwide Airlines, Singapore Airlines, Ukraine International Airlines and US Airways. Executives who are members of the Qualifyer frequent flyer programme can earn points with THY and all of the above airlines.

London: ❑ Tel: +44 207 766 9300
Manchester:❑ Tel: +44 161 489 5289
Chicago: ❑ Tel: +1 312 943 7858
New York: ❑ Tel: +1 212 339 9650
Miami: ❑ Tel: +1 305 577 8187
Rest of US: ❑ Toll free: +1 800 874 TURK (8875)
Dublin: ❑ Tel: +353 137 0011
Montreal: ❑ Tel: +1 514 989 3110
Toronto: ❑ Tel: +1 416 955 8591
Vancouver: ❑ Tel: +1 604 683 7824
Sydney: ❑ Tel: +61 2 9299 8400
Website: [www.turkishairlines.com].

3

A number of other Turkish carriers also operate international flights to the country. These include İstanbul Airlines, Green Air, Sultan Air and Air Alfa. These cater mainly for the tourist market and are largely charter airlines. They therefore serve the main tourist destinations. They do not offer the same level of service as THY.

International airlines

The following international airlines fly regularly to Turkey: British Airways, Delta Airlines (the only US carrier to fly direct to Turkey operates a New York to İstanbul service), Air France, Lufthansa, KLM, Swissair, Olympic and Alitalia.

British Airways

❑ Tel (UK): +44 345 222111, 0345 222747 (Club Class) Website: [www.britishairways.com].

Delta Airlines

❑ Tel: (US toll free) +1 800 221 1212
(UK): +44 0800 414 767
Website: [www.delta-air.com].

Air France

❑ Tel (UK): +44 845 0845 111
Website: [www.airfrance.com].

Lufthansa
Website: [www.lufthansa.co.uk].

KLM
❑ Tel (UK): +44 8705 074074
Website: [www.klm.com].

Swissair
❑ Tel (UK): +44 207 434 7200
Website: [www.swissair.com].

Olympic
❑ Tel (UK): +44 207 409 2400
Website: [www.olympic-airways.gr].

Internal Flights

Please see the relevant city section (Chapter 9) for information on domestic flights.

By Land

By land

Business travellers should think carefully before contemplating driving to Turkey. The country's reputation for poor driving conditions is well deserved and has one of the highest road accident and road death rates in the world. Most Western European car rental firms will not allow their vehicles to be driven into either Turkey or most Eastern European countries that you have to cross to reach Turkey. Business visitors driving their own cars will probably have to purchase extra insurance. However, there are no special bureaucratic requirements for bringing a car temporarily into Turkey. The vehicle's details will be entered in the driver's passport as a temporary import and the car must be driven out of the country by the same person within the permitted time limit, usually three months.

Rail

Travelling to Turkey by train is not a viable option. The service is slow, unreliable and uncomfortable. The famed London-İstanbul Orient Express belongs to the past – these days it only runs as far as Venice.

By Sea

Car ferries link Italy and Greece with Turkey. Services are more frequent in the summer months than in the winter. Most ferries go to tourist destinations and direct ferries to İstanbul are rare.

Customs Procedures

Customs formalities are quite straight forward. The Turkish customs authority operates a green (nothing to declare) and red channel system. The customs allowances include five litres of liquor, 400 cigarettes and one kilogram of coffee. You are supposed to declare unusually expensive jewellery or electronic items such as laptops and video cameras. These are then entered into your passport to ensure that you take them with you on departure. If you are clearly on a business trip and hold a return ticket, you may not even be asked to do this. Most customs inspections are cursory. Samples with a commercial value should also be declared but there is no need to declare samples with no value or literature such as brochures and catalogues.

Customs allocations

You should keep all currency exchange receipts and sales slips for any high value purchases or items that could be mistaken for antiques. On your departure you may be asked to prove that you bought such articles legally. There are harsh penalties for exporting antiques without authorisation. A licence is required for even the smallest article. You may be asked to prove that carpets or other craft items are not antique.

Health

You should ensure that you have adequate travel insurance. There are no inoculation requirements for entering Turkey but you should discuss with your doctor any recommended vaccinations. Bear in mind that air quality in most Turkish cities, especially İstanbul and Ankara, is very poor and this may complicate any existing respiratory problems.

You should take more than enough supplies of any regular medication and a doctor's prescription to prove that you need to take the drugs. Turkey strictly enforces anti-drug smuggling laws and officials may be suspicious of any large quantities of medicines. You should, where possible, keep medicines in their original containers.

Medication

The most likely health problems that you will encounter in Turkey relate to stomach upsets. These can be minimised by drinking bottled water, which is widely available and usually served as a matter of course in restaurants, and eating only freshly prepared and cooked foods. If you do fall ill, Turkey has excellent health facilities and most large hotels have a doctor available on call or can recommend somewhere.

There are two things that usually strike the visitor to Turkey on arrival. The first is the banknotes and the second is the standard of driving. There seems to be an extraordinary number of zeros on banknotes and to repeat visitors there always seems to be more than last time. For the first- time visitor, the drive from the airport to the hotel can be hair-raising and for the seasoned traveller, the standard of driving is always worse than you remember. However, you quickly grow accustomed to both.

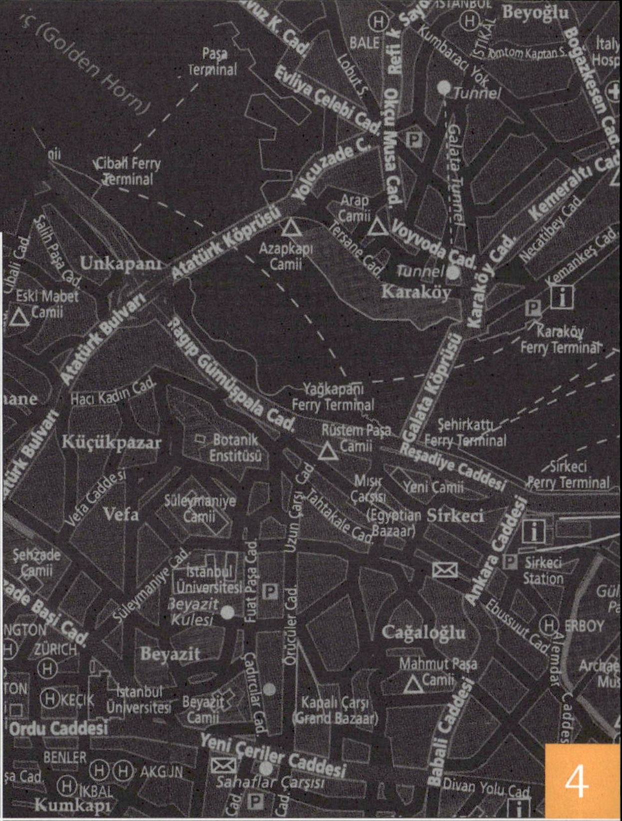

4

the ground rules

4

the ground rules

This section takes the reader by the hand and talks through the nitty-gritty of everyday life, from how to get around to how much to tip the bell-boy. Knowledge of these essentials provides the confidence to go out and do business effectively.

Money

The Turkish Lira (TL) is fully convertible and there is no significant black market. But do, however, watch out for exchange scams. In the 1990s the Turkish lira suffered massive devaluation against the Sterling, US dollar and other major currencies. The exchange rate can alter markedly on a daily basis and it is therefore advisable to change modest amounts of currency frequently rather than a large amount in one transaction. Commission fees are usually modest and therefore you will not lose a great deal in this way. Take a little time to familiarise yourself with the notes and coins. Notes come in denominations of TL100,000, 250,000, 500,000, 1 million, 5 million and 10 million. In practice, you will rarely come across the lower value notes and the 10 million note. The notes between 100,000 and 1 million are the most used, but watch out the 100,000 and 5 million notes are very similar in colour. Coins are replacing the lower value notes and you are most likely to come across coins valued 25,000, 50,000 and 100,000. There are also TL5,000 and 10,000 coins but again you will rarely come across these.

4

Survival: some facts and figures

Currency: Turkish Lira (TL)

Time zone: GMT +2 hours

Flying time from London: 3.45 hours approximately

International dialling code: 90

International access code: 00

EMERGENCY TELEPHONE NUMBERS

ambulance: 112 **fire:** 110 **police:** 155

Electricity: 220 volts, 50 cycles (European style plugs)

Weights & measures: metric system

Currency

The preferred foreign currencies are US dollars and deutschmarks but business executives should face few problems changing other major currencies especially in the larger cities. Traveller's cheques are accepted but many non-bank exchange offices will charge a hefty commission.

It is usually only larger bank branches that offer foreign exchange facilities and accept traveller's cheques. Bank's foreign exchange procedures can be cumbersome and may involve visiting more than one window and lengthy waits. As well as your passport, you may also be asked to produce the original purchase receipt of the traveller's cheques. Bureaux de Change and hotel exchange desks are usually more convenient for cashing traveller's cheques. They may not charge a commission if you are a guest but will probably offer a slightly lower rate than the banks. Exchanging cash is quicker and usually commission free. You should keep all exchange receipts as these may be needed if you want to exchange Turkish Lira for foreign currency at the end of your trip.

Travellers' cheques

Credit cards are widely accepted in Turkey, even by the smallest establishments. However, some shopkeepers may be reluctant to accept payment by credit card for modest sums (say less than the equivalent of $50). The most commonly accepted cards are Visa and Mastercard. American Express is less widely accepted than in many other countries. Automated teller machines (ATMs) linked to international networks such as Cirrus or Plus Systems are common in major cities. Most of the major Turkish banks are also members of Visa and you can obtain cash advances on your Visa card from their numerous ATMs.

Getting Around

As mentioned earlier, driving yourself in Turkey is not recommended. For getting to and from the airport and getting around the main cities, taxi is the best method. At airports, there are organised taxi ranks and cabs use meters for the journey into the city. Avoid taxi touts who try to tempt you away from the official rank. They will demand a flat fare that is far above the going rate. You are also more likely to encounter pirate taxi drivers near major tourist sites. However, the vast majority of drivers are honest and use their meters fairly.

Taxis

It is not usual to tip taxi drivers but the fare is usually rounded up for convenience as finding small change is always a problem. It is also acceptable to round down a fare. At night, fares are 50 per cent higher and the meter will display the word *gece*.

Other forms of public transport in cities such as buses and *dolmus* (a form of taxi that follows set a route and charges a flat fare) are usually crowded and not reliable or efficient enough for business use.

For inter-city travel, the Turkish Airlines (THY) domestic service is the fastest and most convenient method. THY offers an extensive and reliable service to most Turkish cities from hubs in İstanbul and Ankara.

The long distances between most cities make overland travel impractical in many cases. However, there are numerous coach services and many are served by modern and comfortable vehicles. This may be the best option to cities that are relatively near, for example, to Bursa from İstanbul.

It is not advisable to drive yourself on inter-city trips. Speed limits and lane discipline are frequently ignored on inter-city roads, making driving especially hazardous. In addition, few inter-city roads are of the same standard as motorways in Western Europe.

Hotels

There is a wide range of suitable accommodation for business travellers to Turkey. This includes the international hotel chains, locally-owned chains and independent hotels which offer business–standard facilities. Most large cities have a choice of hotels conveniently located for business districts and transport facilities. (see individual city sections in Chapter 8 and 9 for details). Many hotels offer basic business services and modern facilities such as Internet access and mobile telephone hire.

Flashing

In most of the world, flashing your head lights is generally a courtesy showing you will give way. Beware: in Turkey a car flashing its lights is saying: 'Stop! My right of way!'

Communications

Mobile telephones have conquered Turkey. No self-respecting Turkish business executive is without one and they will expect you to be contactable by phone at all times. The major Turkish cities are well-covered by mobile phone networks and mobiles are available for temporary hire. GSM (Global System for Mobile telephones) standard phones are available and operate in Turkey. The biggest mobile telephone company is Turkcell [www.turkcell.com.tr]. It probably has the best coverage in all the major Turkish cities.

Mobile telephones

Using a mobile is the best way of keeping in touch as you go about your business in Turkey although payphones are available and usually work reliably. Payphones usually operate by phone cards available in various values from street kiosks and other shops. International lines are sometimes difficult to obtain.

Turkish hotels, like hotels everywhere, charge a significant mark-up on telephone calls but usually allow freephone numbers so that pre-paid call cards can be used, such as those issued by AT&T, MCI and American Express.

Eating and Drinking

Dining out

Turks are rightly proud of their cuisine and eating out is a popular national pastime. Although the general perception in Western Europe is that Turkish food consists of nothing but kebabs, this is not the case. Vegetables and rice play an important part and vegetarians should experience few problems in finding good food. In many Turkish restaurants, the food is laid out as in a buffet. However, you point out the dishes that you want to the waiter or chef and they are brought to your table. A Turkish culinary institution is *meze*. This is served at the start of the meal and consists of a number of hot or cold dishes that you eat with bread. *Meze* can constitute a meal in itself.

There is an abundance of restaurants serving good quality Turkish food at moderate prices as Turks expect to get value for money when dining out. A meal with wine or beer should not cost you more than the equivalent of US$25 per person. Non-Turkish cuisine such as French, Italian or Chinese tends to be more expensive, with restaurants located either in five star hotels or in upmarket areas. Invitations to either lunch or dinner are a usual part of business negotiations and you will make a good impression if you return the invitation and entertain your business contacts.

The national drink is tea. This is usually served without milk in tulip shaped glasses and sugar is added to taste. You will almost certainly be offered tea at the start of any meeting. The national alcoholic drinkı is *rakı*, a strong aniseed-flavoured drink usually served with water. Despite being an Islamic country, alcohol is widely available and openly consumed. Beer, wine and *rakı* are produced in Turkey. The beer is usually lager (pilsener) and matches the quality of Western European beers. The best Turkish wines are drinkable but are not of the highest standard. The best label is Kavaklıdere, which produces both a white and a red.

Bottled water is widely available and is the best option for consumption. Tap water is safe to drink in most Turkish cities but is heavily chlorinated and can have an unpleasant taste. It may also cause short-term illness in those not accustomed to drinking it.

Watch Out!

Overall, Turkey is a safe country and crime rates in its major cities are lower than in the UK or North America. However, visitors should take a few precautions to avoid falling victim to theft or confidence tricks.

Pickpockets and con artists see foreign visitors as lucrative easy prey. Wealthy-looking foreign executives will attract particular attention. Dress down slightly and avoid valuable watches, jewellery and expensive-looking briefcases. Pickpockets tend to congregate in crowded areas popular with tourists. The minimum amount of time should be spent in areas like markets and a close eye kept on belongings at all times. Where possible, valuables should be kept in the hotel safe and only money necessary for immediate expenses should be carried.

Scams

The most common type of scam concerns foreign exchange. You may be approached in the street and asked if you want to change money. Refuse. If you accept, you will almost certainly be ripped off, either by being given a poor rate or finding that the bundle of 'notes' contains little more than cut up newspaper.

You may also be approached in the street by someone claiming to be a police officer and asking you to hand over your wallet so that the legality of your foreign exchange transactions can be checked. Again, refuse to hand over anything but appear to be willing to co-operate by offering to go to the nearest police station to clear up any misunderstanding. The impostor will flee at this point.

Another scam, once common, appears to have become less frequent. This involved 'spiking' the drinks of unsuspecting visitors with sleeping pills. When the victim woke up, their valuables would have been stolen. This was particularly popular in downmarket bars frequented by backpacking tourists. The rare incidents that do still occur appear to be mainly in tourist areas.

Areas to Avoid

Executives whose business requires a trip to south-east Turkey should seek specialist advice on the latest situation. Kurdish insurgents have long been active in the area. Travel to major cities is safe but the authorities will probably insist on a military escort for overland travel outside urban centres. Business travellers should co-operate fully with the authorities and attempt to spend the minimum amount of time in the area.

Executives should avoid low-income red light districts; *gecekondu* in Turkish. Foreigners wandering into such areas attract attention and face a higher risk of theft or falling victim to the scams noted above.

This chapter takes off its jacket, rolls up its sleeves and gets down to business. It starts with a guide to Turkish business etiquette for men and women and then moves on to practical issues including trade regulations, payment methods, customs procedures and duties. It also includes a section on the 'suitcase trade' and ends with a guide to further sources of information.

Turkey's increasing integration into the European economic system and the global economy means that Turkish executives are accustomed to international business practices and conventions. The first-time business visitor will find few surprises. On the practical side, successive government reforms have greatly simplified business procedures and created one of the most liberal trading regimes in the region. Turkey's customs union with the EU, which came into force on 1st January 1996, has encouraged such liberalisation and continues to be one of the driving forces behind the modernisation of Turkish commercial practices.

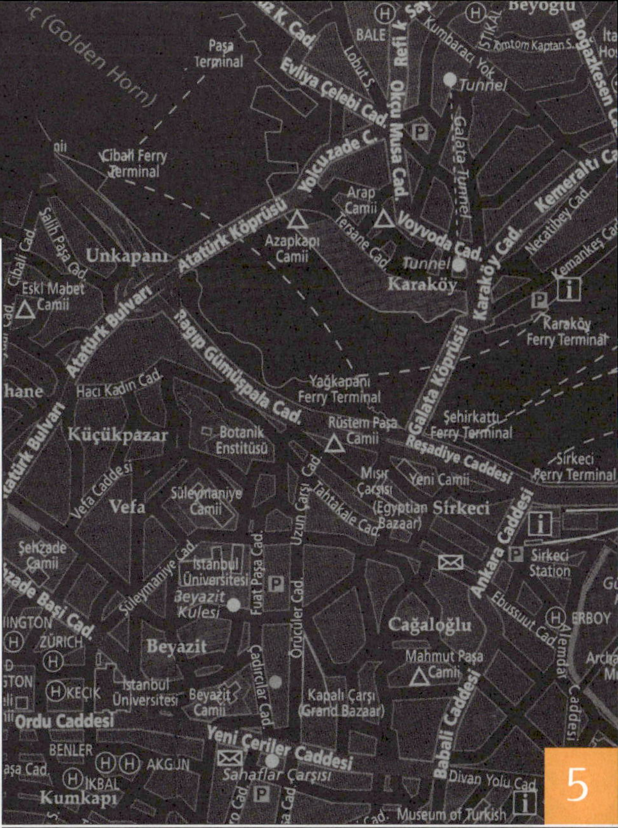

5

getting down to business

5 getting down to business

This chapter provides elementary guidance on the etiquette of the business, and also contains details of useful local organisations who can assist with the more complicated requirements of business transactions.

Business Etiquette

Turks have a well-developed sense of hospitality and business visitors will find their hosts at meetings take good care of them. As in many parts of the Middle East, light refreshments will be offered – usually tea – and some general conversation will take place for up to twenty minutes before any serious discussion gets under way. It is polite to accept the refreshment offered. Visiting executives will find that initial meetings will be quite formal and it is usual to use surnames and titles rather than first names. You may find that your Turkish interlocutors never use your first name and you should continue to use their surnames until otherwise indicated. It is usual to exchange business cards.

You are more likely to meet women in senior positions in Turkey than in many other Middle Eastern countries. Likewise, Turkish business people are accustomed to dealing with women executives who can dress in the same manner as they would at home. As a man, however, it is worth noting that some strict Muslim women might be put out by an attempt to shake hands.

Turkish hospitality

There is a strong sense of patriotism in Turkey. The majority of Turks are justifiably proud of their long history of civilisation and the achievements of the modern Turkish state. There are laws against defaming the Turkish Republic, its founder Kemal Atatürk and the Turkish flag. Even light-hearted remarks concerning the state of the currency may be taken the wrong way. Although you will find that Turks complain about the state of their country and the perfidy of their politicians, you should be wary about agreeing too strongly with them.

Business hours

During the week many businesses open at 8 am (banks at 8.30 am) and close at 5 pm with a break for lunch between 12.30 and 1.30 pm on weekdays. Shops stay open later, usually to 7 or 8 pm or even longer in tourist areas.

The weekend is Saturday and Sunday. Most shops open on Saturday and some main post offices will open Saturday morning. Banks do not open on Saturday or Sunday.

5

Public Holidays

The dates of holidays marked * change every year as these are religious holidays based on the lunar calendar. The dates for 2000-2003 are as follows:

	2000	2001	2002	2003
New Year's Day	**1 Jan**	**1 Jan**	**1 Jan**	**1 Jan**
Kadir Gecesi* (Night of Power – 27th night of Ramadan)	**4 Jan**	**23 Dec**	**12 Dec**	**1 Dec**
Seker Bayrami* (*Eid al Fitr* – end of Ramadan)	**8 Jan**	**27 Dec**	**16 Dec**	**5 Dec**
Kurban Bayrami* (*Eid al-Adha* – end of the pilgrimage season)	**16 Mar**	**5 Mar**	**22 Feb**	**11 Feb**
National Sovereignty Day	**23 Apr**	**23 Apr**	**23 Apr**	**23 Apr**
Youth and Sports Day (in commemoration of Atatürk's Birthday)	**19 May**	**19 May**	**19 May**	**19 May**
Prophet Muhammed's birthday*	**14 Jun**	**3 Jun**	**23 May**	**12 May**
Navy Day	**1 Jul**	**1 Jul**	**1 Jul**	**1 Jul**
Victory Day	**30 Aug**	**30 Aug**	**30 Aug**	**30 Aug**

This is a national holiday but in addition many towns hold a holiday on the date that they were liberated during the War of Independence. For example, Izmir celebrates on 9 September.

Republic Day	**29 Oct**	**29 Oct**	**29 Oct**	**29 Oct**
Anniversary of Atatürk's death. (The whole country stops at 9.05 a.m.)	**10 Nov**	**10 Nov**	**10 Nov**	**10 Nov**

Practical Business Procedures

Turkey's trade regime is increasingly integrated with the Europe; Turkey has introduced the same tariff rates on goods from third countries as apply in the EU. The country also uses many of the same standards and regulations. The customs union means that many goods from the EU can be imported duty free into Turkey. However, Turkey's full membership of the European Union is still a distant prospect.

Since 1983, successive government reforms have encouraged private enterprise and reduced the role of the state in the economy. Foreign executives will find themselves dealing with private sector companies except in obvious areas such as defence procurement and large infrastructure projects. This is good news for business visitors as Turkish private sector companies are on the whole efficient and honest, in contrast with the Turkish public sector which has a reputation for slowness and corruption. Private companies attempt to have as little as possible to do with state-owned enterprises and the state in general.

Trade regulations

This guide can contain only a brief overview of the regulations concerning trade with Turkey. Exporters should first obtain expert advice from chambers of commerce and other relevant organisations.

Import licences

The Turkish government long ago abolished import licences and most goods can now be freely imported into the country. However, certain restrictions still remain. The import of some types of goods is restricted to certain government agencies or needs government permission. The import of alcoholic drinks and cigarettes continues to be a government monopoly held by the government agency Tekel. Firearms, ammunition, along with the material needed to make these items and other hazardous materials, require government approval for their importation. The Central Bank must authorise the import of precious metals and stones. Most chemicals used in the food industry and in the production of medicines along with all medicines for both human and animal use and cosmetics require permission from the Ministry of Health. All goods that require after-sales service including motor vehicles and electronic equipment need the permission of the Ministry of Industry, which must be satisfied that an adequate nationwide spare parts and service network has been established. The Ministry of Environment issues control certificates before certain chemicals and materials can be imported; these include coal, petroleum, arsenic, mercury and scrap metal.

Documentation

Documentation requirements follow the EU system. A commercial invoice, certificate of origin and a bill of lading or airway bill (depending on method of transport) must accompany every commercial shipment. Certification by the appropriate Turkish consular authority of commercial invoices and certificates of origin is required.

Three copies (including the original) of the commercial invoice are required. One copy must accompany the goods and the original should be forwarded to the importer via the appropriate bank. The invoice must contain a complete description of the goods and payment terms. The exporter must also sign the invoice and it must contain the following declaration: 'We hereby certify that this is the first and original copy of our invoice, the only one issued by our firm for the goods herein mentioned.'

Certification

The appropriate chamber of commerce should prepare the certificate of origin in English. Two copies are required. One copy must accompany the goods and be surrendered to the customs authorities on importation. No corrections are allowed to certificates of origin.

Exporters should ensure that the details on the bill of lading or airway bill match precisely the details on all other shipping documents to avoid delays.

A pro-forma invoice may be required to open a letter of credit or to satisfy other credit requirements. Such invoices must be less than six months old at the time of application, contain an unexpired option (if appropriate), note freight and insurance charges separately and contain the importer's name.

Customs procedures

Customs clearance procedures are generally efficient as long as all documents are in order. Import duties, where applicable, are calculated on a cost, insurance, freight (c.i.f) basis. The average level of import duty is around 5 per cent but this is expected to fall to less than 4 per cent as Turkey harmonises its import duty system with the EU. The importer is required to pay VAT (known by its Turkish initials as KDV) after import duty and any other relevant charges have been added. VAT is calculated on a sliding scale from a maximum of 23 per cent, but most goods are taxed at 15 per cent.

The suitcase trade

Since the collapse of the Soviet Union and the end of the Eastern bloc, Turkey has become an important trading partner of many of these former Communist states. Much of this commerce is informal and is known as the 'suitcase trade'. Eastern European and former Soviet nationals bring goods – often in suitcases, hence the term – to Turkey to sell and use the proceeds to buy electronic and other luxury goods to take back home. Although informal in the sense that much of the trade is neither taxed nor subject to official regulation, it has become highly organised and a lucrative source of income for Turkey. The government is therefore reluctant to interfere. Many of the suitcase traders travel to Turkey on coaches, and whole coach companies depend for their income on these entrepreneurs. The coach companies have attempted to secure a tighter grip on the market by constructing service areas along the routes (both in Turkey and in the destination countries) where their vehicles stop for fuel and refreshments. The Turkish Central Bank estimates that the informal sector may be half as large again as registered economic activity and that 'suitcase trade' exports would add around 20 per cent to the country's export total.

Payment

Customs duty

Letters of credit with terms of between thirty and ninety days are the normal payment method in Turkey. Exporters should only accept more liberal payment terms from well-established customers with a good credit track record. The use of letters of credit reduces the risk of non-payment or late payment. This has become of greater concern in the aftermath of the two earthquakes in Turkey in late 1999. Many companies hit by the disasters will be forced to use capital to rebuild premises and defray other costs.

Further information

A detailed description of documentation and other requirements for exporting to Turkey is in Dun & Bradstreet's *Exporter's Encyclopaedia*. For contact details *see* page 32. D&B also produce a monthly analysis of payment risk in over 85 countries, including Turkey. For a sample, visit [www.uk.dnb.com/prodserv/int-r-p].

5

Turkish government ministries

General Directorate for Foreign Investment of the Undersecretariat of Treasury
Eskisehir Yolu
İnönü Bulvari
Emek Mevkii
Ankara
❑ Tel: +90 312 212-8800; fax: +90 312 212-8916
E-mail: [gdfi@pm.treasury.gov.tr]
Website: [www.treasury.gov.tr].

Ministry of Industry and Commerce
Tandoğan
Ankara
❑ Tel: +90 312 231 7280; fax: +90 312 286 5325

Ministry of Health
Yenisehir
Ankara
❑ Tel: +90 312 431 2486; fax: +90 312 433 9885

Ministry of Environment
İstanbul Caddesi, 88
İstikler
Ankara
❑ Tel: +90 312 342 3900; fax: +90 312 285 2742

Central Bank of Turkey
Istiklal Caddesi, 10
06100 Ulus
Ankara
❑ Tel: +90 312 310 3646; fax: +90 312 310 7434
Website: [www.tcmb.gov.tr]

Chambers of Commerce

Turkish-British Chamber of Commerce and Industry
89 Goswell Road
London, EC1V 7ER
❑ Tel: +44 207 336 0686; fax: +44 207 336 0696

Union of Chambers of Commerce, Industry, Maritime Commerce and Commodity Exchanges of Turkey
Atatürk Bulvari, 149
06640 Bakanlıklar
Ankara
❑ Tel: +90 312 418 3360; fax: +90 312 418 3268

İstanbul Chamber of Commerce
Rağip Gümüspala Caddesi, 84
34378 Eminönü

İstanbul
❑ Tel: +90 212 511 4150; fax: +90 212 526 2197
Website: [www.tr-ito.com].

İstanbul Chamber of Industry
Meşrutiyet Caddesi, 118
80050 Tepebaşı
İstanbul
❑ Tel: +90 212 252 2900; fax: +90 212 249 3963

Chamber of Maritime Commerce
Meclisi Mabusan Caddesi, 22
80154 Sali Pazari
İstanbul
❑ Tel: +90 212 252 0130; fax: +90 212 293 7935

Ankara Chamber of Commerce
Eskişehir Yolu
Soğutozu
Ankara
❑ Tel: +90 312 286 4036; fax: +90 312 286 3446

Ankara Chamber of Industry
Atatürk Bulvari, 193/4
Kavaklıdere
Ankara
❑ Tel: +90 312 417 1200; fax: +90 312 417 2060

İzmir Chamber of Commerce
Atatürk Caddesi, 126
35210 Pasaport
İzmir
❑ Tel: +90 232 441 7777; fax: +90 232 483 7853

Adana Chamber of Commerce
Sadyam Caddesi, 67
Adana
❑ Tel: +90 322 359 7872

Turkish Industrialists and Businessmen's Association (TUSIAD)
Meşrutiyet Caddesi, 74
80050 Tepebaşı
İstanbul
❑ Tel: +90 212 249 1929; fax: +90 212 249 1350

YASED (Association for Foreign Capital Co-ordination)
Barbaros Bulvari
Morbasan Sokak
Koza İş Mekezi B Blok/Kat 1

80700 Beşiktas
İstanbul
❑ Tel: + 90 212 272 5094; fax: + 90 212 274 6664

5

6

industry overviews

6

industry overviews

An overview on each of the major industries of the nation, and where they stand today.

Turkey is a remarkable economic success story registering the highest average annual economic growth of all OECD countries in the 1990s. The country has recorded this strong growth in recent years despite internal and external challenges. These have included high levels of inflation and investor wariness of emerging markets following crises in Asia, Russia and Brazil. Turkey suffered its own financial crisis in 1994-5 but the underlying robustness of the economy meant that it weathered that storm better than many in the Turkish business community expected.

The Turkish economy has undergone considerable change since the then prime minister Turgat Özal embarked on economic liberalisation in 1983. Although agriculture remains an important economic activity, the country has developed a diverse manufacturing base and a sophisticated service sector. A massive population shift has also occurred with mass migration to the cities, especially İstanbul. This has placed a heavy burden on infrastructure and municipal services. Overall, the population is richer and living standards have risen. A large, Western-oriented and well-educated middle class has emerged. Turkey's economic success and the opportunities it offers has resulted in it becoming a prime target for export initiatives by Western governments. The US Commerce Department have designated Turkey one of its 'Big Ten Emerging Markets' and it is in the top twenty export markets for British companies. Germany, Italy and France are important trading partners.

Contacts

Prime Minister's office for the South-Eastern Anatolian Project (GAP)
Uğur Mumcu Sokak, 59
06700 Gaziosmanpaşa
Ankara
❑ Tel: +90 312 446 9722; fax: +90 312 437 6777

Foreign Economic Relations Board (DEIK)
Istiklal Caddesi, 286/9
Odakule, Beyoğlu
İstanbul
❑ Tel: +90 212 243 4180; fax: +90 212 243 4184

Turkish Industrialists and Businessmen's Association (TUSIAD)
Meşrutiyet Caddesi, 74
80050 Tepebaşı
İstanbul
❑ Tel: +90 212 249 1929; fax: +90 212 249 1350

YASED (Association for Foreign Capital Co-ordination)
Barbaros Bulvari
Morbasan Sokak
Koza İş Mekezi B Blok/Kat 1
80700 Beşiktas, İstanbul
❑ Tel: +90 212 272 5094; fax: +90 212 274 6664

Energy

6

Hydro-electricity

Turkey has huge future energy needs because of its rapidly growing economy and lack of development in this sector. Energy demand is growing at around 10 per cent per year. To satisfy this demand, 2,000–2,500 megawatts of capacity will have to be added every year for the next 10–15 years. Although Turkey has already invested heavily in hydro-electric schemes, notably the South Eastern Anatolian Project (known by its Turkish initials **GAP)** in south-east Turkey, future electricity generating capacity will come from natural gas fired stations. The country is therefore set to become a major importer of natural gas. Gas consumption is set to grow from its current level of 10 billion cubic metres per year to more than double that in 2005 and nearly triple in 2010. Various schemes have been proposed to satisfy this demand by importing gas from neighbouring countries such as Russia and Iran as well as from further afield from Egypt, Jordan and Turkmenistan.

Oil

In addition, Turkey is set to become one of the most important transit countries for the export of oil from Azerbaijan. The favoured route for the main export pipeline enters Turkey from Georgia and terminates at the Mediterranean port of Ceyhan.The so-called Baku-Ceyhan pipeline has been the object of much discussion and negotiation since Azerbaijan first gained independence from the Soviet Union and invited foreign companies to participate in its oil industry. Although Azerbaijan has considerable oil resources, explorations since independence have not proved as fruitful as first believed.

This, combined with uncertainty over oil prices during the 1990s and unresolved boundary disputes in the Caspian Sea, has acted to hinder agreement on the route of oil export pipelines. The construction of any export pipeline will require massive investment and the commercial feasibility of the Baku-Ceyhan pipeline has yet to be confirmed. This project will take some time (possibly many years) to come to fruition due to the complex interplay of commercial and political factors.

Export pipelines

The GAP Project

The GAP project is actually a collection of separate grand projects to build dams across the rivers Tigris and Euphrates and their tributaries. The project was first conceived in the 1950s and much of it has been completed. The project has created hydroelectric plants and made more land available for cultivation through irrigation as well as encouraging the development of industries.

The latest phase of the project envisages the construction of the Ilisu dam across the river Tigris and has created considerable controversy, particularly in the UK where the government has promised substantial sums in aid. The controversy surrounds the damaging effects on the local population and sites of historic interest. The lake created by the dam will flood several towns and inundate sites of archaeological interest. The forcible removal of the affected populations has raised concerns about abuse of human rights. Most of the population is Kurdish and there are suspicions that political as well as economic motives underlie the removals. The damming of the rivers Tigris and Euphrates is also opposed by countries downstream – Syria and Iraq – as it will significantly reduce the flow of much needed water.

Turkey's future needs for gas has led it to seek numerous sources. Turkey has agreements with Russia, Iran, Turkmenistan, Egypt, Qatar, Nigeria and Iraq for the supply of gas. Most of these are only framework agreements and do not legally commit Turkey to buy any gas. The only two legally binding agreements are with

Russia and Iran. Turkey also wants to ensure that it does not become reliant on one supplier. Turkey obtains 7 per cent of its current gas requirements from Russia. The agreement with Iran commits Turkey to buying 10bcm per year via a pipeline that is under construction.

Gas pipelines

As well as the Iranian pipeline project, the other major proposals for satisfying Turkey's gas needs are:

Transcaspian pipeline (TCP). This plan envisages bringing gas from Turkmenistan via a pipeline along a route through Azerbaijan. The group behind the plan is the Pipeline Services Group (PSG), which is a consortium involving BP Amoco, Bechtel and GE Capital. Before the plan can be realised, major investment would have to be undertaken in the Turkmen gas industry in order to ensure reliable gas supplies. In addition, Turkmenistan and Azerbaijan would have to resolve a dispute over their mutual border in the Caspian Sea. This proposal added to the complication surrounding the Baku-Ceyhan oil export pipeline proposal – would it complement the pipeline? The discovery of significant gas resources in Azerbaijan after the launch of the TCP proposal is also an added complication, as Azerbaijan's attitude towards the plan altered. Turkmen gas would compete with its own gas.

Blue Stream. This plan envisages the construction of a pipeline across the Black Sea to supply Russian gas to Turkey. Construction contracts were awarded to the Italian company Saipem in early 1998. The project will have to overcome significant technical difficulties. The pipeline will be the deepest sub-sea gas pipeline ever constructed. In addition, the soft seabed of the Black Sea and the particularly corrosive nature of the water in the Black Sea will increase these difficulties . This project risks reinforcing Turkey's dependence on Russia for its gas supplies.

Egypt. This is the least developed of the specific plans to supply Turkey's gas needs and will need to overcome considerable political obstacles before it can make progress. The plan envisages constructing a pipeline from Egypt via Jordan and Syria with spurs supplying those markets as well as the Palestinian areas and possibly Israel. This is one of the many grand projects to have emerged from the regional peace process and may never come to fruition.

Others. Plans to supply Iraqi gas to Turkey will have to wait until after UN sanctions against Iraq have been dismantled and considerable investment has been undertaken in Iraq's yet-to-be-developed gas industry.

Plans to supply gas to Turkey from more distant sources such as Qatar and Nigeria will rely on liquefied natural gas (LNG). This will require the construction of new facilities to de-liquefy the gas on arrival. These plans remain no more than proposals and little concrete action has been taken.

Investment opportunities

For those seeking to break into Turkey or to increase their role, all this activity in the energy sector presents ample opportunities. These opportunities range from investment in large-scale projects such as the construction of power plants or pipelines to the supply of materials, equipment and services to support these projects. Requirements exist within the entire energy production cycle from power generation to consumer supply. The Turkish government is keen to encourage private (including foreign) investment in this sector in the form of build, own, operate, transfer (BOOT) contracts. There is also ample scope for the expansion of exports to satisfy demand in this sector. Foreign imports account for the majority of supplies to the sector and are estimated to reach around US$1.5bn in 1999 (a 13 per cent increase on 1998).

Contacts

Ministry of Energy and Natural Resources
Konya Yolu
06100 Bestepe
Ankara
❑ Tel: +90 312 213 6601; fax: +90 312 223 6984

Turkish Electricity Distribution Company (TEDAS)
İnönü Bulvari, 27
06440 Bahcelievler
Ankara
❑ Tel: +90 312 212 6915; fax: +90 312 213 8873

Turkish Electricity Generation and Transmission Company (TEAS)
İnönü Bulvari, 27
06440 Bahcelievler
Ankara
❑ Tel: +90 312 222 9536; fax: +90 312 222 9890

Turkish Petroleum Corporation (TPAO)
Mustafa Kemal Mahallesi, 2
Cadde, 86, 06520 Esentepe
Ankara
❑ Tel: +90 312 286 9100; fax: +90 312 286 9000

Petroleum Pipeline Corporation.(BOTAS)
Bilkent Plaza, A3 Blok
Bilkent
Ankara
❑ Tel: +90 312 266 0700; fax: +90 312 266 0623

Telecommunications

As well as investment in its energy needs, Turkey also requires huge investments in its communication and transport infrastructure. This investment has already started with new roads, airports and telephone networks. Turkey's large size and its growing population will demand continuing investment and expansion in these services for several years to come.

6

Telecommunications is another sector in which strong economic performance is driving rapid expansion. Although, Turkey possesses a modern telecommunications infrastructure, it still lags behind Western standards with telephone density standing at around 27 per cent and mobile telephone density at less than 4 per cent. Demand for modern services such as the Internet and cable television means that massive investment is needed in the sector. The government has attempted to attract investment by the partial privatisation of the state telecommunications company, Turk Telekom, and the offering of two additional licences to operate mobile telephone networks. There are already two networks in operation.

The massive investment envisaged in telecommunications again augurs well for foreign companies wanting to exploit opportunities in Turkey. Although Turkish companies can manufacture much of the equipment that will be required, there is still considerable room for imports. The size of the market is expected to grow at a much faster rate than the energy sector. There is demand for a wide range of telecommunications equipment from payphones to satellite earth stations, wireless technology and sophisticated equipment for scientific and military use (see also below, Defence). The market was worth an estimated US$830m to foreign companies in 1999 but this represents more than a 50 per cent increase on 1998.

Contact

Ministry of Communications and Transportation
Bahcelievler Son Durak
Emek
Ankara
❑ Tel: +90 312 212 4632; fax: +90 312 212 4187

Environment

Environmental awareness is growing in Turkey and in recent years the government has introduced a series of stringent measures to assess and limit the environmental impact of industrial activity. There are strict regulations on waste disposal and major initiatives in place to upgrade the solid waste and sewage systems in major cities. Pollution control is also a prime concern. Air quality is very poor in major cities, particularly İstanbul and Ankara, and is one of the first things noticed by people when they arrive.

Pollution control

This is another area of Turkish life where the reality has failed to keep pace with the regulations and the level of enforcement. Although strict regulations exist on waste disposal, they are often ignored.

The need for advanced technology and the relative inexperience of Turkish companies in this sector create opportunities for foreign companies. Equipment and services such as consultancy are in demand.

Contact

Association of Practitioners of Environmental Technology
Irfan Bastug Caddesi, Yuva Apt 3/10
80280 Gayrettepe
İstanbul
❑ Tel: +90 212 272 2904; fax: +90 212 272 2904

Media

Turkey's media sector is one of the most dynamic in the country. The sector did not really exist before 1990 and has since grown into a multi-billion dollar sector and will grow even further. In 1990, the son of the then Turkish President Turgat Özal launched the first private television channel broadcast by satellite from Paris. Since then, television stations have mushroomed and there are now 16 national channels and over 250 local channels along with over 1,000 radio stations. There is no longer any need to broadcast by satellite from foreign countries. The government acknowledged in 1992 that it could not stem the tide of private television channels and legislated to end the government's monopoly over broadcasting. Most of the channels are free-to-air and gain revenue from advertising. There is one pay TV channel – Cine 5- and a growing network of cable television providers.

Digital networks

Cable television is available in 44 major cities and town. Turk Telekom have plans to expand this network but Turkey's large size presents challenges to rapid expansion of the network. The first digital television provider started broadcasting in 1999 and again Turk Telekom has plans to expand the capacity for digital television services such as pay-per-view and video-on-demand.

Television Regulation

The rapid growth in the media sector has outstripped the government's ability to regulate the sector effectively. As mentioned, the government was forced to abandon the state monopoly on broadcasting in the face of a direct challenge from the private sector and powerful commercial interests. The government only set up a television and radio regulator in 1994. This body, known by its Turkish abbreviation RTUK, has still to license the allocation of broadcasting frequencies. Private broadcasters simply appropriated frequencies when they set up without paying licence fees to the government. Efforts by the government to impose licence fees retrospectively have been blocked by lack of legislative time, changes in government and lobbying from media owners.

Although there are laws governing television ownership to prevent concentration of control and cross-ownership with other media, these are not strictly enforced. Two of the major channels are owned by newspaper groups. The ATV channel is owned by the

Sabah newspaper group and Kanal D belongs to the same stable as the Hurriyet and Milliyet publications. Foreigners are barred from owning more than 20 per cent of a television station and this limit is strictly enforced. The major television stations are owned by major conglomerates that exercise considerable political power. Politicians rely on television to get their message across (newspaper readership is low) and the media owners in turn rely on politicians to prevent burdensome regulation. Media barons have therefore become politically powerful and have succeeded in preventing strict enforcement of the regulatory regime. However, the multiplicity of channels and pressure for advertising revenue is likely to encourage consolidation in the sector.

Football coverage

Soccer rights - the golden goal

The most popular programmes on Turkish television are live broadcasts of the top Turkish soccer teams. These regularly attract larger audiences than other programmes due to the country's obsession with soccer. The television channel that has the rights to domestic soccer matches has a huge commercial advantage. It will gain huge audiences and therefore can earn lucrative advertising revenue. In 1998, the pay television station Cine 5 signed an exclusive deal with the top Turkish soccer division for broadcast rights, thereby securing access to the most lucrative games. An alliance of ATV and Kanal D attempted to circumvent this agreement, which runs until 2001, signing individual deals with two of the top clubs. The battle went to court, which ruled in Cine 5's favour. All the major national channels will engage in a fierce struggle to gain rights to broadcast domestic soccer when they become available in 2001. The channel that is successful will win a huge commercial prize.

Television

The popularity of television has made it the most important medium for advertising. The conglomerates that own television stations use their control to advertise their other products at deeply discounted rates (even free in some cases). In 1998, advertising spending amounted to around $1.5bn but over $6bn worth of airtime was sold according to published rate cards. The competition for advertising expenditure between the channels is fierce and this has also led to discounting. The advertising airtime purchase business is divided between two companies MEPAS, which sells time for Show TV, one of the largest channels, and BIMAS which sells airtime for ATV and Kanal D. The other major channel, Star TV, has separate arrangements.

Transport

Transport Infrastructure

This is another sector where economic growth has lead to rapidly expanding demand. Turkey needs the transport infrastructure to take advantage of this growth. The large size of the country means that goods and people often need to be moved over long distances and it needs more than one transport hub. The government is encouraging private investment in the construction of new airports, ports and roads, again through BOT contracts. İstanbul's international airport has been upgraded recently under a BOT scheme and a new airport for the Asian side of the city is proposed. The expansion of port facilities at İzmir and Mersin has also been put forward. Most overland travel is by road rather than rail but Turkey has relatively few Western standard motorways. The exception is the İstanbul-Ankara highway. To cope with projected increases in road traffic, significant investment in new roads will have to be undertaken. The large-scale nature of many of these projects again creates many opportunities for the supply of a wide range of materials, equipment and services. Road vehicles are already one of the UK's top exports to Turkey despite the country having its own manufacturing capability.

Textiles

Textiles are Turkey's main overseas earner, accounting for almost 40 per cent of total exports. The country is the fifth largest cotton producer in the world and the sixth largest textile producer. The removal of quotas for EU exports under the 1996 customs union boosted the sector and led to investment of over US$1bn. Most of Turkey's needs can be met from local sources and imports of foreign machinery and other goods are declining. These imports were worth around US$1bn in 1999, so the sector remains an important market but foreign companies should not expect future expansion in demand.

Contact

Turkish Clothing Manufacturers' Association
Yıldız Posta Caddesi
Dedeman İş Hani 48/8
80700 Gayrettepe
İstanbul
❑ Tel: +90 212 274 2525; fax: +90 212 272 4060

Defence

Although the Cold War is over, Turkey remains a key member of NATO, as demonstrated by its role during the 1999 conflict in Kosovo and its continued support for the containment of Iraq. Large-scale purchases and projects are particularly vulnerable to political factors and undergo extensive reviews before being given the go ahead. The government realises the political influence it can wield through its defence procurement activities and has demonstrated a willingness to use it. The Turkish Ministry of Defence is thought to have operated a policy of denying defence procurement contracts to companies whose governments have criticised its human rights record, especially with regard to the conflict in the south-east. German and French companies, in particular, are believed to have fallen victim to this policy. There is not thought to be any bar on British or US companies.

The Military

The military is one of the core national institutions and military service is compulsory for all males. Turkey possesses the second largest standing army in NATO and has the highest military spending in NATO as a percentage of GDP. Foreign companies supply most of the military's needs from sophisticated hardware to basic items.

Contacts

Ministry of National Defence
Mudafaa Caddesi, Bakanlıklar
Ankara
❑ Tel: +90 312 418 9616; fax: +90 312 417 7342

Defence Industries Manufacturers' Association
Çankaya Caddesi, 16/3
06680 Çankaya
Ankara
❑ Tel: +90 312 440 5566; fax: +90 312 440 5567

Tourism

Tourism is one of Turkey's prime earners of foreign currency with receipts equivalent to around 3 per cent of GDP. The sector has undergone rapid expansion in the past two decades and this is set to continue. The combination of historic sites, impressive scenery and Mediterranean beaches makes the country a highly desirable holiday destination. The type of package on offer is expanding beyond the traditional beach holiday to niche markets including activity based holidays centred on sailing, fishing, skiing and other sports. The continued success of the sector requires massive investment to develop new sites and upgrade existing facilities. There is considerable scope for foreign companies through the supply of materials, equipment and professional services.

Holiday sports

6

The main tourist areas are the Aegean coast (with resorts such as Bodrum and Marmaris) and the western Mediterranean coast around Antalya along with İstanbul. Airports at İzmir and Dalaman serve as gateways for the tourist industry as well as İstanbul. Impressive sites at Ephesus and Pamukkale can also be reached from the coastal resorts. The other frequently visited area is the region of Cappadocia in the Anatolian interior, south east of Ankara. Turkey's long history and wide variety of landscapes offer the opportunities to develop tourist facilities throughout the country. The opportunities in this sector impinge on many other key sectors. Transport and utility infrastructure will have to be upgraded to cope with the increasing numbers of tourists. The government is also keen to ensure that tourism development is conducted in a sustainable manner that does not endanger the environment. The government is implementing the $3bn Mediterranean-Aegean shoreline tourism project (ATAK) to protect 4,000 km of coastline and ensure delivery of basic services such as drinking water and waste disposal to meet tourist needs in a sustainable manner.

Beach resorts

Contacts

Ministry of Tourism
İnönü Bulvari, 5
06100 Emek
Ankara
❑ Tel: +90 312 212 8300; fax: +90 312 212 8590

Union of Travel Agents of Turkey (TURSAB)
Gazeteciler Sitesi, Haberler Sokak, 15
Esentepe
İstanbul
❑ Tel: +90 212 275 1361; fax: +90 212 259 0656

Tourism Investors Association
Cumhuriyet Çaddesi, Çelik Apt 235, Kat 3
80230 Elmadağ
İstanbul
❑ Tel: +90 212 234 5245; fax: +90 212 231 1845

Union of Turkish Hotel Operators (TUROB)
Mete Caddesi, Mete Palas, 26/2
Taksim
İstanbul
❑ Tel: +90 212 249 5153; fax: +90 212 252 1664

Construction

As well as infrastructure projects such as airports, ports, roads, power plants and pipelines, there is strong demand for new housing, retail premises and office space. Turkey's population is expected to reach 87 million by 2010; this will require around 7.3 million new houses in that period. The sector is worth around US$5bn. This is good news for foreign companies wanting to supply goods and services to this sector.

Imports are on an upward trend but still account for a small part of the total market as local firms have considerable expertise and can supply most local needs. Turkish construction firms are of international standard and compete successfully in global markets. Foreign companies still have the edge when it comes to supplying specialist products and services, especially those involving advanced technology. The two earthquakes in late 1999 demonstrated the twin requirements of high building standards and advanced technology to reduce damage in future earthquakes.

Contacts

Contractors Association of Turkey
Ahmet Mithat Efendi Sokak, 21
96550 Çankaya
Ankara
❑ Tel: +90 312 439 1712; fax: +90 312 439 4621

Mass Housing Association
Gazeteciler Sitesi, Yazarlar Sokak, 28/3
80630 Esentepe
İstanbul
❑ Tel: +90 212 275 6695; fax: +90 212 275 6696

Agriculture

Agriculture once dominated the Turkish economy but has declined in relative importance. The sector still accounts for around 13 per cent of GDP and continues to be a major employer; around 40 per cent of the population are employed in agriculture related activities. The sector has received two substantial boosts in recent years. The first is the GAP hydro-electric project, which is intended to increase substantially the amount of agricultural land; the government is keen to create modern irrigation-fed farms that use the latest technology. The second is the opening of the EU to Turkish produce under the 1996 customs union. These factors mean that imports of agricultural machinery and other goods are on the increase after years of decline. The best opportunities for foreign companies lie in specialist goods and services as local companies can meet most general needs.

Contacts

Ministry of Agriculture, Forestry and Rural Affairs
Milli Mudafaa Caddesi, 20
Kizilay
Ankara
❑ Tel: +90 312 417 8400; fax: +90 312 425 2016

Food Industrialists Association
Tuna Caddesi, Halk Sokak, 20/7
Yenişehir
Ankara
❑ Tel: +90 312 431 1685; fax: +90 312 431 2704

Consumer Goods

Turkey has seen an explosion in demand for consumer goods in recent years as living standards have risen with economic success. Demand for well-known international brands is particularly high. International companies have partly satisfied this demand by establishing franchise operations in the country. The first was set up by McDonalds in 1986 and it has been followed by a number of others particularly in the fast food and fashion sectors. The turnover of franchise operations is expected to reach US$2bn by 2000. The government is keen to encourage franchise operations in most sectors and treats them in the same way as foreign investment. This allows companies access to substantial incentives. Electronics is booming with the growth in ownership of goods such as mobile phones, televisions, personal computers and stereos.

Contacts

IT Association of Turkey
Selanik Caddesi, 17/4
06650 Kızılay
Ankara
❑ Tel: +90 312 418 4755; fax: +90 312 425 4817

Electronic Equipment Manufacturers' Association
Yıldız, Barbaros Bulvari
Sakir Kesebir Sokak, 34
80700 Beşiktaş
İstanbul
❑ Tel: +90 212 266 0290; fax: +90 212 272 4711

Electronic Industrialists' Association
Bagdat Caddesi, 477/4
81070 Suadiye
İstanbul
❑ Tel: +90 216 386 0909; fax: +90 216 386 0910

Other Important Industries

Other key sectors providing substantial opportunities for foreign companies include the automotive industry, healthcare and security.

Turkey has a well-developed motor manufacturing capability but needs to import around 65 per cent of the components needed to supply this industry and the spare parts market. Most motor manufacturers are also undertaking modernisation and expansion programmes. There is also a need for imported vehicles, as locally based firms cannot satisfy the entire market.

Healthcare

The healthcare market is another sector that has expanded considerably in recent years. The number of private hospitals increased by around 50 per cent in the period 1993–8. Turks are demanding ever more sophisticated treatment. This is a market that provides significant opportunities for foreign companies.

Security equipment

Although crime rates remain below those found in Western European and North American countries, they have increased in recent years. The risk of terrorist attacks has also greatly reduced in recent years but there is still some danger. Demand for security equipment and services has therefore increased. Most buildings have some form of security guard and many have installed sophisticated entry-control, monitoring and alarm systems.

Contacts

Automobile Importers' Association
Yenitarlabaşi Caddesi
Guzel İzmir Apt 20/3
Taksim
İstanbul
❑ Tel: +90 212 288 6184; fax: +90 212 275 7069

Automotive Manufacturers' Association
Atilla Sokak, 6
81190 Altunizade
İstanbul
❑ Tel: +90 216 318 2994; fax: +90 216 321 9497

Chamber of Medical Doctors
Turkocaği Caddesi, 17, Kat 3
Cağaloğlu
İstanbul
❑ Tel: +90 212 522 1911; fax: +90 212 522 7374

Turkish Dental Association
Meşrutiyet Caddesi, 32/8
Yenişehir
Ankara
❑ Tel: +90 312 417 7492; fax: +90 312 417 1922

7

how to set up a permanent operation

7

how to set up a permanent operation

This section does not set itself up as the be-all and end-all reference for establishing an office. Its aim is to provide a sweeping overview for the visitor who is considering the possibility of a local office. The following pages highlight some of the pitfalls and benefits, give an insight into the legal situation, and run through some of the major issues to be considered, such as recruiting, finding premises, etc.

Turkey's location on the edge of Europe and close to the Middle East, Africa and Central Asia makes it ideal as a permanent base to exploit these markets. It has also become a favoured location base for Asian firms wanting to exploit the European market. For European companies, it offers significantly lower labour costs while Turkey's 1996 customs union with the EU and its acceptance in 1999 as a candidate for full membership mean that Turkish-produced goods have excellent access to European markets. Turkey is a large and increasingly sophisticated market in its own right. The country's economic development in the last two decades and its growing prosperity have fuelled demand for foreign goods and services; many companies have found the best way to take advantage of these opportunities is to establish a permanent presence in the country.

The complex interplay of vested interests, nationalist sensitivities, language and cultural barriers combined with concerns about physical safety and political instability have deterred some companies from fully exploiting commercial opportunities in Turkey. There are strong links between major business interests, politicians and organised crime in some sectors. This has led to the perception of widespread corrupt practices and that vested business interests have enjoyed political protection. This combined with a strong sense of nationalism has often obstructed the entry of foreign companies into the Turkish market. However, whilst there are risks for companies seeking to establish a permanent presence in the country they are not as significant as may be first perceived. Turkey's frequent changes of government in the mid to late 1990s reinforced the country's reputation for political instability. The general direction of government policy has, however, changed little: it has remained pro-liberalisation and Western-oriented. The private business sector has developed strategies for dealing with instability and for bypassing the corruption that appears to exist in some sections of the public sector; primarily by minimising contact with the government and the bureaucracy. However, foreign companies establishing an operation in the country will have to deal with the government and negotiate Turkey's complex public administration.

Joint-ventures

The most common strategy that foreign companies use to reduce the risks to their operation in Turkey is to find a reliable Turkish partner and establish a joint venture. Although 100 per cent foreign ownership of commercial operations is permitted under Turkish law (*see* p.87 Legal and Regulatory Framework), in practice very few foreign companies take advantage of this. A joint venture brings several key advantages including a local name, access to existing infrastructure such as distribution networks and a partner who knows the local business environment and how to avoid the pitfalls. Foreign companies should not rely totally on their Turkish partner for a picture of the local market and, as noted earlier in this guide, should conduct thorough research of their own. This should include research into the potential partner to ensure that there are no skeletons in the closet.

The need for due diligence: a case study

A European company was presented with an opportunity to invest in a Turkish leisure operation and saw this as a good opportunity to expand its overseas portfolio. One of the directors was, however, concerned by press reports that some leisure operations in Turkey were fronts for organised crime and that to address the problem theTurkish government was considering changing the laws concerning ownership of such operations. The company did not want to be associated with organised crime and was concerned that any legal changes would affect its legitimate investment. It therefore called in outside consultants to investigate both its potential partner and the prospect for changes in the law. The consultants found that while the potential partner company probably did not have any direct links to organised crime syndicates, it had close connections to political figures who were suspected of such links and of corruption. The consultants also established that moves to change the law were well advanced but would not prevent foreign companies taking legitimate stakes in a Turkish operation. The company decided to delay its investment until the new law came into effect and to find a new partner. This strategy was vindicated by a subsequent successful investment in a Turkish leisure company with a good local reputation. The original partner company did in fact become embroiled in a scandal regarding its political connections.

Legal and Regulatory Framework

Turkey possesses one of the most liberal foreign investment regimes in the region and actively encourages foreign involvement in most sectors of the economy, although companies wanting to take advantage of the opportunities continue to face bureaucratic hurdles and legal obstacles. The courts have blocked some large infrastructure projects after campaigns on environmental and other grounds. There is some suspicion that local vested interests have orchestrated such campaigns to keep out foreign competition.

Although foreign investment is regulated by a law dating back to 1954, this has been updated, most recently in 1995, to take account of modern business practices. Turkish law provides adequate protection for foreign companies and their operations in the country, in theory treating foreign and domestic firms equally. In practice, foreign businesses in dispute with a Turkish company will soon discover that nationalist sensitivities do play a part and may find it difficult to obtain a favourable judgement against a Turkish entity, especially one with good connections. Although, as previously noted, 100 per cent foreign ownership of businesses is permitted, there are exceptions: broadcasting, where foreign companies are allowed to own a maximum 20 per cent of an individual company, and aviation and maritime transport, where the limit is 49 per cent.

Foreign ownership

The text of current laws and regulations governing foreign investment can be read at: [www.treasury.gov.tr/english/invest.htm].

Licences to conduct commercial operations are granted by the General Directorate of Foreign Investment (GDFI) at the Undersecretariat of Treasury. The form of company organisation used will depend on the size of the operation. Large concerns may opt for public listing as a *Anomin Sirket* (AS), which is roughly equivalent to plc status. Alternatives for smaller operations are a private limited company or a branch office. Applications must be made in writing to the GDFI to start a new business or to invest in an existing one. Each partner must invest a minimum of US$50,000 in cash or kind. It is also possible to establish a liaison office in Turkey. Such offices are not allowed to undertake revenue generating business and their costs must be met from foreign currency transferred from abroad.

Raising capital

Companies that engage in commercial operations in Turkey are free to repatriate profits, dividends, capital and other payments as long as the applicable taxes have been paid. Turkey has a sophisticated and well-regulated banking system through which such transfers can be made and finance raised, although foreign companies are likely to find the interest rates applied to business loans punitive and may find raising finance at home or in a third country a better option. The full range of professional advisors such as accountants and lawyers exists in Turkey, including representatives of international firms.

Franchise operations

Franchise

Under Turkish law, franchising operations are considered in the same category as foreign investment. The Turkish authorities welcome franchising operations as a useful method of creating jobs and transferring know-how and modern business methods to Turkey. The General Directorate of Foreign Investment (GDFI) regulates franchising operations by foreign companies. The relevant law is the 1984 Foreign Capital Incentive Law 6224 and the subsequent 1986 Decree 86/10353. Under these laws franchise applicants must provide: a draft of the franchise agreement; documentary evidence of the physical facilities to be used in the franchise operation; a feasibility report; information on the foreign company such as turnover and assets; patent information, if applicable.

Royalties from franchise operations can be transferred abroad after a 10 per cent tax deduction.

Local Employees

Turkish Workers

Foreign companies establishing a permanent presence in Turkey will have little difficulty recruiting a capable workforce. Turkish workers have a well-deserved reputation for hard work and reliability. Education standards are high and many Turks have received at least some education abroad, mainly in Europe. Labour costs, including wages, are lower than in much of Europe and this is one of the country's attractions for foreign companies. Turkish workers have grown accustomed to international business practices through their long exposure to foreign companies operating in the country. Familiarity with modern technology is high especially in urban areas. However, foreign businesses may find that they still have to conduct extensive internal training programmes, especially in more rural areas.

With few exceptions, Turkish workers are no longer inclined towards militancy and industrial relations have been good in recent years. Union membership is strong, especially in the private sector; public sector workers have only recently been allowed to join unions. Companies are legally obliged to negotiate in good faith with recognised trade unions. Strikes are rare, and when they do occur are usually short-lived.

Expatriates

Most major Turkish cities provide very comfortable postings for expatriate families and facilities are good. Standards of housing, utilities, shops and other amenities are comparable to Europe and expatriates rarely have to make radical changes to their lifestyles. International schools also exist in the larger cities such as İstanbul and Ankara.

Air pollution

The most significant inconveniences arise from transport problems and air quality. The traffic congestion that blights most major Turkish cities and the poor standard of public transport can make getting around on a daily basis difficult. In addition, most major Turkish cities suffer from air quality problems. The situation in İstanbul and Ankara (especially the latter in winter) is particularly acute. At best the poor air quality causes some discomfort, at worst it can have serious consequences for those with asthma, other respiratory or heart conditions. Those who believe they may be vulnerable should consult their doctor before undertaking a posting to Turkey.

Suburbs

Traffic fumes are a major cause of this air quality problem, and massive traffic jams as workers try to get to the office or factory in the morning can mean long journey times for expatriates who usually live in the smarter suburbs on the edge of major cities.

In İstanbul, the main residential areas for expatriates are the suburbs strung out along the European shore of the

Expatriates

Bosporus, north of the city. Expatriate residents report that the journey into central İstanbul (such as the Taksim Square area) regularly takes over an hour and a half in a car for a journey of usually less than twenty miles. The advantages of living in such areas are better air quality and easy access to shopping facilities (the out-of-town supermarket has arrived in force) as well as a higher standard of accommodation and lower crime rates.

In Ankara, the main expatriate residential areas are to the south of the city. Although closer to the city centre and the main government district than the equivalent areas in İstanbul, the same problems of traffic congestion still apply. Again the advantages of such suburbs are better air quality and a higher standard of living. Ankara's suburbs have crept up over the hills surrounding the city and into the valleys beyond in order to escape the pollution.

Location

The location of your operation in Turkey is one of your most vital decisions. For many companies, İstanbul is the logical place to establish an office. It is Turkey's commercial capital and has the best developed business infrastructure. Like all business cities, it also has disadvantages in the form of higher costs (including rents), traffic congestion, crowding and strained utilities.

For those companies hoping to gain significant business from the government, an office in Ankara must be a serious proposition. The city has all the advantages of a capital city in terms of infrastructure and facilities. In terms of costs, Ankara is quickly catching up with İstanbul and, as noted above, suffers from many of the same environmental problems.

Free zones

The economic sector in which you are engaged will also figure in the decision on location. For shipping-related businesses, İzmir or one of Turkey's other main ports will be the logical base. However, much of Turkey's maritime industry is centred in İstanbul. Tourism-related companies may consider locating in one of Turkey's main tourist destinations outside İstanbul such as Bodrum, Marmaris or Antalya. Industrial companies should consider bases in the industrial heartland east of İstanbul, perhaps Bursa (especially the automotive sector) or Izmit.

Turkey also has ten free trade zones and ports, which provide all the usual advantages including exemptions from taxes and duties. For offshore finance companies or those businesses using Turkey as a regional distribution base, these may provide the most attractive location.

Contacts

General Directorate of Foreign Investment (GDFI)
Eşkisehir Yolu
İnönü Bulvari
Emek Mekvii
Ankara
❑ Tel: +90 312 212 8800; fax: +90 312 212 8916
E-mail: [gdfi@pm.treasury.gov.tr]
Website: [www.treasury.gov.tr].

National Franchise Association
Ergenekon Caddesi
Pangalti İş Merkezi 89/15
80240 Pangalti
İstanbul
❑ Tel: +90 212 296 6628; fax: +90 212 224 5130

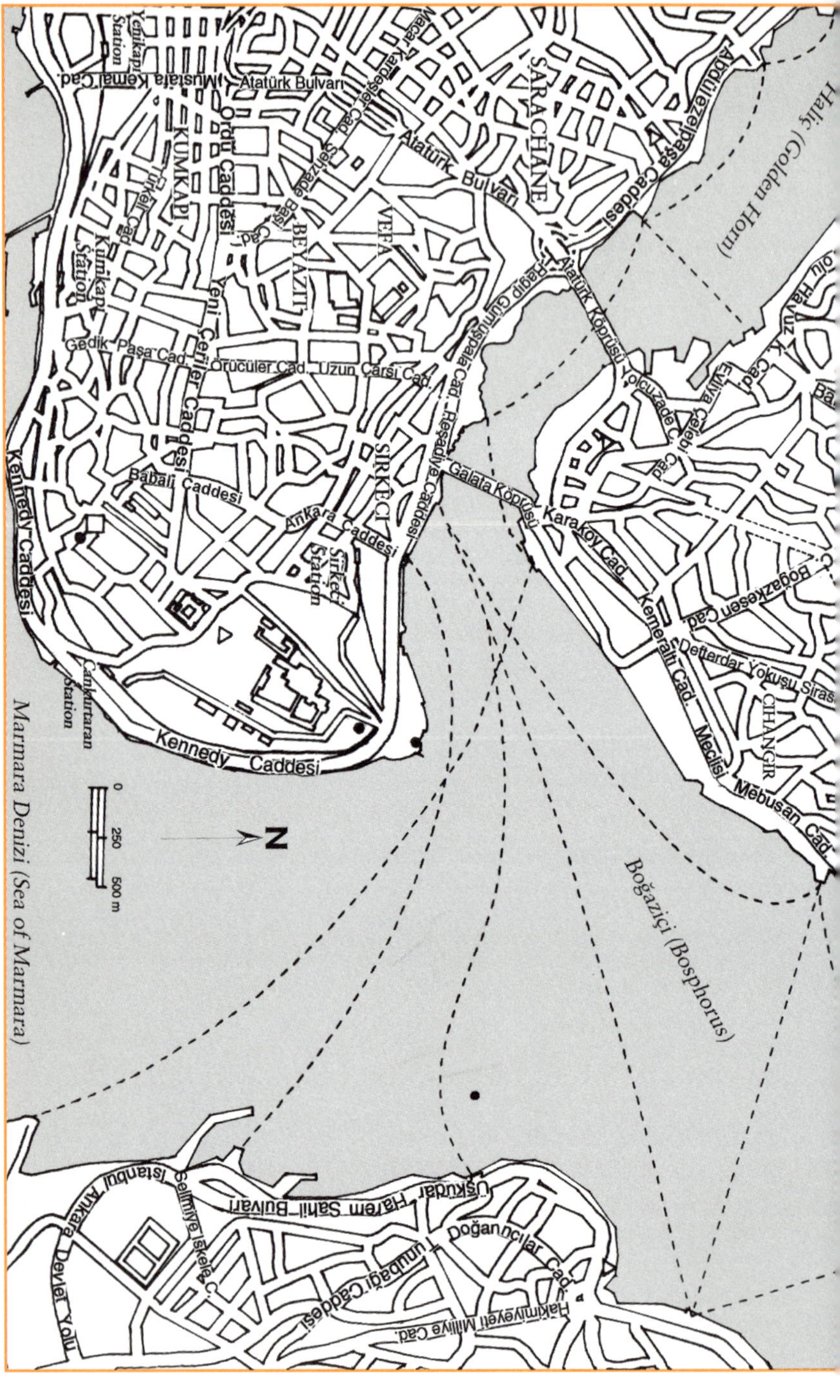
Haliç (Golden Horn)
Abdülezelpaşa Caddesi
SARAÇHANE
Macar Kardeşler Cad.
Atatürk Bulvarı
Şehzade Başı Cad.
VEFA
BEYAZIT
Yenikapı Station
Mustafa Kemal Cad.
Ordu Caddesi
KUMKAPI
Türkeli Cad.
Kumkapı Station
Yeni Çeriler Caddesi
Gedik Paşa Cad.
Örücüler Cad.
Uzun Çarşı Cad.
Ragıp Gümüşpala Cad.
Atatürk Köprüsü
Reşadiye Caddesi
SIRKECI
Babıali Caddesi
Ankara Caddesi
Sirkeci Station
Kennedy Caddesi
Cankurtaran Station
Kennedy Caddesi
Galata Köprüsü
Karaköy Cad.
Yolcuzade C.
Evliya Çelebi Cad.
Havuz K. Cad.
Boğazkesen Cad.
Kemeraltı Cad.
Defterdar Yokuşu Sırası
CIHANGIR
Meclisi Mebusan Cad.
Marmara Denizi (Sea of Marmara)
N
0 250 500 m
Boğaziçi (Bosphorus)
Üsküdar Harem Sahil Bulvarı
Doğancılar Cad.
Selimiye İskele C.
İstanbul Ankara Devlet Yolu
Tunusbağı Caddesi
Hakimiyeti Milliye Cad.

İstanbul

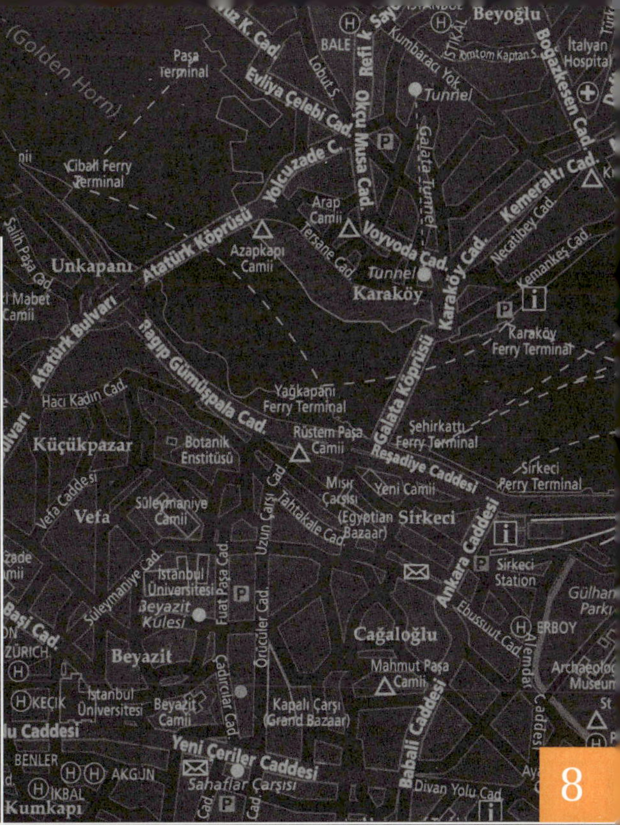

8

İstanbul:the business capital

8

İstanbul

commercial capital

Overview

Although no longer the political centre of Turkey, İstanbul remains the undisputed commercial capital. Many companies have their head offices in or near the city and it is home to the stock exchange and other important commercial organisations. The city is the largest in Turkey and is justifiably proud of its long history.

Early settlement

The site of present day İstanbul was probably first settled around 1000 BC by fishing communities; a village called Lygos is known to have existed on the site now occupied by the Topkapı Palace. By 700 BC Greek colonists had settled on the Asian shore of the Bosphorus. The first significant settlement was established in 657 BC by a Greek colonist named Byzas and the city he founded was named Byzantium. Before leaving Greece, Byzas had consulted the famous Delphi oracle on where to found his new city and was told 'opposite the blind'. On sailing up the Bosphorus, Byzas saw the Greek settlement on the eastern (Asian) bank and looking across to the opposite shore noticed the superb anchorage provided by the Golden Horn. The colonists, he decided, must have been blind not to see the harbour and, in keeping with the Delphic prediction, Byzas built his city on the banks of the Golden Horn.

Byzantium

Byzantium became a willing part of the Roman empire but was all but destroyed by Septimius Severus in 196 AD in revenge for Byzantium's opposition to him in the civil war that had gripped the empire. He eventually rebuilt the city. In AD 342, the Emperor Constantine defeated a rival nearby and declared the city to be the 'New Rome' and in AD 330, the city, renamed Constantinople, became the new imperial capital. It was to remain the capital of the Byzantine empire for over a thousand years, except for a brief period in the first half of the thirteenth century when it was captured by the soldiers of the Fourth Crusade and ruled by Western Europeans. By 1453, the Byzantine empire had been reduced to a small area immediately surrounding Constantinople. The Ottoman Sultan Mehmet captured the city in a daring assault that involved hauling boats overland from the area now occupied by the Dolmabahçe Palace, over the hill where the Hilton Hotel now stands, to the Golden Horn. The city, renamed İstanbul, was the capital of the Ottoman empire until the establishment of the Turkish Republic. In 1923 Ankara was declared the capital of this new state, ending over 1,500 years for İstanbul as a major capital on the world stage.

Istanbul's location

İstanbul is unique in many ways, not least as the only city to span two continents. The European and Asian halves are divided by the Bosphorus which runs roughly north–south through the city and links the Sea of Marmara with the Black Sea. The European half is further divided by the Golden Horn. The main business districts, hotels, consulates and sights of interest are located on the European side. The outskirts of the Asian side and the Asian portion of İstanbul province form part of one of Turkey's main industrial areas.

Arrival

İstanbul is the main gateway for those arriving by air and is well served by international airlines; unlike other Turkish cities, including Ankara. It is the main hub for Turkish Airlines (THY), although for many business visitors there is little need to visit any other Turkish city.

Airport

İstanbul's **Atatürk International Airport** (formerly known as Yesilkoy) is modern and contains all the facilities that you would expect. It has three terminals: international, domestic and charter flights. The airport is well signposted in English and Turkish. Announcements are made in Turkish, English and a language appropriate to the flight.

Visitors who need to purchase a **visa** before passing through immigration can do so at a booth to one side of the immigration hall. The baggage collection carousels are located immediately after immigration.

Foreign exchange

There are *bureaux de change* facilities both before and after customs. There is little difference in the exchange rates offered. Check your money carefully before leaving the counter as some clerks have been known to take advantage of traveller's disorientation and unfamiliarity with the currency to short change new arrivals. Such incidents are rare and most clerks will carefully count out the money in front of you.

Airport taxis

The airport is located on the European side of the city and the journey into town takes 20–30 minutes depending on the time of day and your exact destination. The quickest and most convenient method is by taxi. There is an official rank at the terminal exit.

You should only take cabs from this rank and ignore taxi touts. The fare into the city centre should be the equivalent of US$10–20, again depending on the time of day and the exact destination. The taxis should use the meter.

Business class hotels in İstanbul do not usually offer a complimentary shuttle service but can arrange for you to be met and the cost charged to your bill.

Accommodation

İstanbul has a good selection of business class hotels. Most of the top international chains are represented in the city but there is also a good selection of more modestly priced hotels, which offer adequate facilities for the business traveller. Most of these hotels are located in the area centred on Taksim Square to the north of the Golden Horn. Many offices are located in this area and this makes it particularly convenient. The hotels in the Taksim area frequently offer rooms with a view of the Bosphorus at a premium. Asking for a room without a Bosphorus view can bring the room rate down. Other areas of İstanbul that the business traveller is likely to visit are only a short taxi ride away. There are also some suitable places to stay in the Sultanahmet area where the city's main tourist attractions are located.

Around Taksim Square

Hilton ★★★★★
Cumhuriyet Caddesi
❑ Tel: +90 212 231 4650; fax: +90 212 240 4165
Website: [www.hilton.com].

Located on a hill about three blocks from Taksim Square itself, the Hilton is set in its own park and has all the facilities that you would expect in a five-star hotel including business centre, gym, swimming pool and jogging track. Rooms on the Bosphorus side have spectacular views.

Hyatt Regency ★★★★★
Taşkişla Caddesi
❑ Tel: +90 212 225 7000; fax: +90 212 225 7007
Website: [www.hyatt.com].

Located one block closer to Taksim than the Hilton, this hotel also offers all the facilities expected in a five-star hotel.

Ceylan Intercontinental ★★★★★
Taksim Parkı
❑ Tel: +90 212 231 2121; fax: +90 212 231 2180
Website: [www.interconti.com].

This hotel towers above Taksim Square, next door to the Hyatt Regency.

Divan ★★★★★
Cumhuriyet Caddesi
❑ Tel: +90 212 231 4100; fax: +90 212 248 8257

This locally owned independent hotel is dwarfed by its better-known rivals in the area but offers the same level of service. It is located just two blocks north of Taksim in front of the Hyatt Regency.

Marmara ★★★★
Taksim Square
❑ Tel: +90 212 251 4696; fax: +90 212 244 0509

Another locally-owned independent hotel, the Marmara matches the international chains in level of service and price. It is located on Taksim Square, which is a busy interchange at all hours. Rooms on the square side of the hotel can therefore be noisy.

8

Pera Palas ★★★★★
Meşrutiyet Caddesi
❑ Tel: +90 212 251 4560; fax: +90 212 251 4089

The *grande dame* of İstanbul hotels, it was built in the 1890s to cater for the needs of Western European visitors brought to İstanbul by rail. It retains many original fittings and has a certain faded glory. Each room bears a distinctive name-plate to commemorate a famous visitor who has slept there – Agatha Christie amongst them. The service and the quality of the restaurant no longer match international standards. Although the hotel is moderately priced by İstanbul standards, guests are paying for a sense of history more than anything else. However, the bar or pastry shop are useful places to arrange to meet people.

Richmond ★★★★★
Istiklal Caddesi
❑ Tel: +90 212 252 5460; fax: +90 212 252 9707

A moderately priced respectable hotel whose nineteenth century façade hides a modern hotel popular with American visitors.

Mercure ★★★★★
Mesrutiyet Caddesi
❑ Tel: +90 212 251 4646; fax: +90 212 249 8033
Website: [mercure/istanbul/ index.html]

Located opposite the Pera Palas, the Mercure is more modern and offers a higher standard of service at much the same price.

The hotels listed below are located on the Bosphorus shore. They all belong to international chains and offer the usual facilities.

Çirağan Palace Kempinski ★★★★★
Çirağan Caddesi
❑ Tel: +90 212 258 3377; fax: +90 212 259 6687

A former Ottoman palace which has been sympathetically converted into a hotel. Its history, location and level of service make this a contender, with the *Four Seasons*, for the best hotel in İstanbul.

Conrad International ★★★★★
Yıldız Caddesi, Besiktas
❑ Tel: +90 212 227 3000; fax: +90 212 259 6667

In keeping with other Conrad Hotels, one of the finest in the five-star category.

Swissôtel
Bayıldım Caddesi, Maçka, Beşiktaş
❑ Tel: +90 212 259 0101; fax: +90 212 259 0105
Website: [www.swissotel.com].

This is a modern hotel near the Bosphorus shore with all the facilities to be expected from a top class business hotel. Its location is a little inconvenient for getting to some of the main business centres, but taxis are readily available.

Sultanahmet

This is the area bordered by the Golden Horn to the north and the Bosphorus to the east. It is the oldest part of İstanbul and is where many of the city's most famous landmarks are located. Hotels catering for tourists rather than business executives dominate the area.

Four Seasons ★★★★★
Tevkifhane Sokak
❑ Tel: +90 212 638 8200; fax: +90 212 638 8210
Website: [www.fshr.com]

Located in a restored Ottoman building almost next door to the Aya Sofya, in the heart of ancient İstanbul. It is much smaller than many Four Seasons hotels, having only sixty-five rooms. One of the best hotels in İstanbul.

Arcadia ★
Dr Imren Oktem Caddesi
❑ Tel: +90 212 516 9696; fax: +90 212 516 6118

This is the only other business standard hotel in the area. It is modern and moderately priced.

Ottoman houses

There are a number of converted Ottoman houses in the Sultanahmet area which offer modern comfortable accommodation for business executives. These establishments have limited numbers of rooms and offer something more individual and intimate than the large hotels. Although levels of service match the best hotels, these premises may not have the full range of business facilities.

8

Yeşil Ev
Kabasakal Caddesi, 5
Tel: +90 212 517 6785; fax: +90 212 517 6780

Mavi Ev (Blue House)
Dalbastı Sokak, 14
❑ Tel: +90 212 638 9010; fax: +90 212 638 9017
E-mail: [bluehouse@istanbulhotels.com]

Ayasofya Pansiyonlari
Soğukçeşme Sokak
❑ Tel: +90 212 513 3660; fax: +90 212 513 3669
E-mail: [ayapans@escortnet.com.tr]

Getting Around

Taxi is the most convenient method of transport for most journeys in İstanbul. Taxis are plentiful and easily identifiable; you should have little trouble hailing one on most main streets at most times of the day. The fare starts at around the equivalent of US$1.25. The maximum you should pay for a journey in central İstanbul is around US$5. Journeys to the airport and more distant places will be more.

If your business takes you to the Asian side of the city, the most convenient way to cross the Bosphorus is on one of the many ferries or catamarans. These offer a quick and frequent service. You buy your ticket at a booth at the ferry terminal. Beware of touts attempting to sell tickets away from the booths. On the other side, catch a taxi to your destination.

Other forms of public transport, such as buses can be crowded and inefficient.

Eating and Drinking

İstanbul has the full range of restaurants from fast food snack bars through to top class establishments serving the highest standard of Turkish and Western European cuisine. This range exists in both the Taksim and Sultanahmet areas of the city. It is not possible to list all of the restaurants in these two areas let alone the whole city, so the restaurants below act as a guide only. All the hotels listed previously have good restaurant facilities. New restaurants are opening all the time and others closing, so the best option may be to ask local contacts for a recommendation.

Around Taksim Square

Istiklal Caddesi, which runs for around a mile and half south-west from Taksim Square, contains a multitude of restaurants serving Turkish cuisine, both in the street itself and in the side streets which run off it. One of the better restaurants is **Haci Baba** on the first floor of number 49. Further down the street and just off it on Sakizağaci Sokak is **Haci Abdullah**, one of the best known restaurants in the area. This restaurant does not serve alcohol, probably as it is next door to a mosque. Both are typical Turkish restaurants.

If you are looking for a more impressive restaurant in the area, there is the **Boğaziçi Borsa** at the convention centre next to the Hilton Hotel. This serves modern Turkish cuisine in elegant surroundings. The restaurant at the **Divan Hotel** is also well known for its European and Turkish cuisine. The hotel's pub also serves food.

Sultanahmet

As you would expect in the city's main tourist centre, there is a vast number of restaurants in the area. These primarily cater for the tourist market and can get very crowded at meal times. The most famous restaurant is the **Pudding Shop** on Divan Yolu, the main street that runs west from Sultanahmet Square. This is no longer the hippie hangout that it once was and has become respectable, if overpriced and a magnet for tourists. It gets very crowded. Next door is the smarter **Sultan Pub**. This has a bar and café on the ground floor and a restaurant on the first floor. The restaurants at the **Arcadia Hotel** and **Mavi Ev** are worth a visit for their views of the city as well as the standard of food.

Other recommended restaurants

Rami
Utangaç Sokak, 6
❑ Tel: +90 212 517 6593

Behind the Sultan Ahmet mosque in a restored Ottoman house, the Rami also has fine views of the city from its rooftop terrace.

Daruzziyafe
Meydani, 27
❑ Tel: +90 212 518 1351

Located on the Hippodrome just to the right of the Sultan Ahmet mosque.

Rumeli Cafe
Ticarethane Sokak, 8
❑ Tel: +90 212 512 0008

This is a restaurant as well as a café. It is located just north of Divan Yolu.

Other areas

There are numerous seafood restaurants of varying quality along the Bosphorus to the north of İstanbul. Many of these have a real atmosphere, with traditional folk singers circulating between the tables and excellent Turkish cuisine. It is best to get a local recommendation for these.

Time off

In İstanbul, the main sites in the Sultanahmet Square area can be seen in a day. These include the Topkapı Saray, Aya Sofya, the Sultanahmet Mosque and the underground cistern.

The **Topkapı Saray** will take half a day in itself, especially if you include a tour of the harem. The Topkapı was the palace of the Ottoman sultans.

Highlights include the collection of china and kitchen equipment, the treasury and Islamic holy relics. Tickets for the harem tour are in addition to the entrance fee and are sold from a booth next to the harem entrance. If you have the time, the tour is worth taking to see the impressive decoration of the apartments and to find out what really went on in the harem.

Aya Sofya is one of the oldest and most impressive buildings in İstanbul and dominates the northern side of Sultanahmet Square. Having served as both a church and a mosque, it is now officially a museum and an entrance fee is charged. For a full history and explanation of the building, visitors should get hold of a good tourist guidebook. It is alternatively known by its Latin name Sancta Sophia or its Greek name Hagia Sofia. Emperor Justinian (527- 65AD) ordered the construction of the original building and intended it as the greatest church in Christendom and, up until the conquest of İstanbul in 1453, it served that role. It was completed in 548 AD but has been rebuilt several times in its long history having suffered earthquake damage and neglect. After the Ottoman conquest the building was converted into the empire's main mosque. As the building was oriented towards Jerusalem, the Islamic additions are slightly off-centre and disrupt the building's symmetry. A *mihrab* (prayer niche) to show the direction of Mecca was built slightly to the right of the alter. A *mimber* (pulpit) was also constructed and huge roundels displaying the names of the Prophet Muhammad, the names of the first four Caliphs of Islam and other prominent figures in early Islamic history were put in place. In addition, the Christian mosaics were covered with plaster. These are now being uncovered and the best examples can be seen on the gallery that runs around the building.

The **Sultanahmet Mosque** is still a place of worship and you should respect Islamic sensibilities when visiting. This includes wearing modest clothing (for both men and women) and removing your shoes at the entrance. Women should cover their heads. You should avoid visiting during prayer times or disturbing those at prayer.

The entrance to the underground **Cistern** (called Yerebatan Saray in Turkish) is on Divan Yolu, which runs westward from Sultanahmet Square. This is now a museum and an entrance fee is charged. Originally built by the emperor Justinian, this huge underground complex housed the city's water supply. The combination of water, light, music and hundreds of columns and arches provide a mysterious and enchanting atmosphere. This site is often overlooked by tourists but is as impressive as any of the palaces or mosques in the city.

If you find yourself with additional time, then other sights of interest include the Covered Bazaar and the Egyptian Market, known as the Spice Bazaar, the Dolmabahçe Palace on the banks of the Bosphorus and the **Süleymaniye Mosque**. The latter is located on top of one of İstanbul's hills west of Sultanahmet and is one of the city's most famous landmarks. It was built on the orders of Sultan Süleyman at the height of Ottoman power and is one of the finest examples of Ottoman architecture in the city. This also is an active mosque.

The **Dolmabahçe Palace** was built in the last years of the Ottoman empire and was intended to match the magnificence of European royal palaces. The Dolmabahçe promises a great deal and has become a popular spot on the tourist trail but usually disappoints. The entrance fee is one of the highest in any museum in İstanbul and is hard to justify. An additional fee is payable to use a camera in the palace. The interior is too dark and visitors should leave their cameras at the ticket booth. Visitors must go on an organised tour, which lasts up to 90 minutes. Queues to join the organised tour can add another hour or more at the height of the tourist season. After paying the high fee and queuing, visitors can be very disappointed. The interior is extravagantly decorated in an attempt to mirror European nineteenth century palaces and there are few original works of art or furniture. There are more appealing sights to visit in the city.

If you want to spend a more relaxing day, then there are boat tours up the Bosphorus from the EmInönü ferry terminal. The excursions leave twice every morning and the round trip takes up to six hours. This includes a two-hour stop for lunch. Avoid the touts at the terminal attempting to persuade you to get on their boats. Some of these boats may be unsafe or you may be stranded halfway up the Bosphorus when the boat owner demands more money for the return trip. Swissôtel and Çirağan hotels have also boat tours with dinner on board, and these are ideal for businessmen and families.

If you are in İstanbul at the right time, the city's **International Music Festival** is staged from late June to mid July and features most styles of music. Programmes and tickets are available from the Atatürk Cultural Centre on Taksim Square. The area is also home to several other theatres and cinemas. The **İstanbul International Film Festival** is held from mid April to early May. Again, details are available from the Atatürk Cultural Centre.

In İstanbul, the main shopping areas are around Taksim Square, particularly Istikal Caddesi and of course the famous Covered Market which is about a mile west of Sultanahmet Square. This is where the images of crowded souks and haggling come to life. Any romanticism will soon be dispelled by the sight of credit card signs on every shop door and stall. The best place for spices, nuts and Turkish Delight is the Egyptian Market.

Useful contacts

Attatürk Cultural Centre
Taksim Square
❑ Tel: +90 212 251 5600; fax: +90 212 245 3916

Consulates
UK
Meşrutiyet Caddesi, 34
Tepebaşı
❑ Tel: +90 212 293 7545; fax: +90 212 245 4989
E-mail: [brcgist@verisoft.com.tr]

USA
Meşrutiyet Caddesi, 104-108
Tepebaşı
❑ Tel: +90 212 251 3602; fax: +90 212 267 0057

Australia
Tepecik Yolu, 58
80630 Etiler
❑ Tel: +90 212 257 7050; fax: +90 212 257 7054

Canada
Büyükdere Caddesi, 107/3
Bengun Han, 3rd Floor
Gayrettepe
❑ Tel: +90 212 272 5174

Ankara
N
0 250 500m
0 250 500yd
Yeni Mah. Bel. Fen. Md.
Celal Bayer Bulvari
Hipodrom Cad.
İstanbul Cad.
Atatürk Cultural Centre
Kazim Karabekir Cad.
Bahçelievler Cad.
Şerefli S.
Ergin S.
Anit Cad.
Anit Kabir
Atatürk Mausoleum
Gençlik Cad.
Turgut Reis Cad.
Kubilay S.
Gazi Mustafa Kemal Bulvari
Celal Bayer Bulvari
Station
19. Mayis Stadium
Cumhuriyet Bulvari
Atatürk Sports Hall
Talat Paşa Cad.
Concert Hall
Gençlik Parki
Opera House
İstiklal Cad.
Ankara Palace
Şinasi S.
Roman Baths
Çankari Cad.
Temple of Augustus
Column of Julian
Hisaparki Cad.
Şehit Teğmen Kalmaz S.
Hasircilar
Kosova S.
Denizciler Cad.
Atatürk Bulvari
Adliye Sarayi
Ethnography Museum
Hacattepe Üniversitesi
Loros S.
Strazburg Cad.
Cihan S.
Necatibey Cad.
Abdi İpekçi Parki
Tuna Cad.
Kurtuluş Parki
Umut S.
Kibris Cad.
Taşkent S.
Dedeefendi S.
Erdem S.
Cemal Gürsel Cad.
Yeni Acun S.
Talat Paşa Cad.
Ulucanlar Cad.
Samanpazari (Bazaar Quarter)
Museum of Anatolian Civilizations
Alladin Camii
Aslanhane Camii
Hacı Bayram Camii
Bentderesi Cad.
Cankiri S.
Altindağ Cad.
Merkez Cezaevi
Ses S.

Ankara

9

other cities

9

other cities

Ankara

Ankara has been the official capital of Turkey since 1923 but has a long history as shown by the Roman and other remains found in the city. It has expanded rapidly in recent years and is now the second largest city in the country. All the government institutions and foreign embassies are located in the city. Business executives dealing with the government in any form will almost certainly have to visit Ankara at some point. The city is well connected to other parts of Turkey by air and land.

The government buildings, embassies, hotels and main commercial districts are located in central and southern Ankara, the area bounded in the north by Cemal Gursel Caddesi and Celal Bayar Bulvari. The city is bisected north–south by Atatürk Bulvari and many key institutions are located close to this main street.

Arrival

A more limited number of international airlines serve Ankara than serve İstanbul but THY has frequent services from many other Turkish cities including fifteen daily flights from İstanbul. The flight takes 1 hour.

9

Ankara's **Esenboğa Airport** is located north of the city and is well-equipped but smaller than İstanbul airport. It is vulnerable to bad weather in the winter, especially fog, and this can cause extensive delays. However, the airport is able to cope with heavy snowfalls and icy conditions.

Those arriving on international flights and needing a **visa** can buy one from a booth just before immigration control.

There is an official taxi rank at the terminal exit and taxis will use their meters for the journey. The cost of the trip into the city should be around the equivalent of US$25 and will take 30-40 minutes depending on the time of day.

By land, the journey from İstanbul takes six to seven hours along a newly built multi-lane highway. Buses are frequent and comfortable.

Accommodation

Ankara possesses its fair share of international chain and independent business standard hotels. All of these are located in central southern Ankara. All provide the business services that you would expect.

Hotels

Hilton ★★★★★
Tahran Caddesi, 12
❑ Tel: +90 312 468 2888; fax: +90 312 468 0909
Website: [www.hilton.com]

Located in the heart of Ankara's embassy district and close to government ministries.

Sheraton ★★★★★
Noktali Sokak
❑ Tel: +90 312 468 5454; fax: +90 312 467 1136
Website: [www.sheraton.com]

This is the landmark cylindrical building, a few blocks south of the Hilton.

Best ★★★★
Atatürk Bulvari, 195
❑ Tel: +90 312 467 0880; fax: +90 312 467 0885

An independent, four-star hotel. It has adequate business facilities and is located across the road from the US Embassy.

Tetra Konur
Konur Sokak, 58
❑ Tel: +90 312 419 2946; fax: +90 312 417 4915

Another four-star independent hotel that provides a respectable level of service. It is located two blocks east of Atatürk Bulvari and about a quarter of mile north of the Best.

Getting around

Taxis are plentiful on most main streets and offer the most convenient method of getting around the city. A journey to most places in central Ankara should cost no more than the equivalent of US$3 during the daytime and 50 per cent more at night.

Other forms of public transport, especially the buses, are usually crowded and do not offer a reliable service.

Eating and drinking

As befits a capital city, Ankara has a wide range of restaurants suitable for business entertaining. Most of these are found in central and southern areas of the city. As well as the restaurants located at the city's business standard hotels listed above, other suitable restaurants include:

Yakamoz
Tunalı Hilmi Caddesi, 114/J 2-3
Kavaklıdere
❑ Tel: +90 312 426 2752

Specialises in seafood.

Yeni Hamsiköy
Besteker Sokak, 78
Kavaklıdere
❑ Tel: +90 312 427 7576

Another seafood restaurant, just off Tunali Hilmi Caddesi to the north of the Yakamoz.

Villa
Boğaz Sokak, 13
Kavaklıdere
❑ Tel: +90 312 427 4148

Located behind the Sheraton hotel, the Villa serves European style food rather than typical Turkish cuisine.

Time off

In Ankara, the 'must see' site is Atatürk's mausoleum, on one of the city's hills. It is known as **Anıt Kabir** and, in any case, your hosts may take you there. As well as a large mausoleum housing Atatürk's tomb, there is a museum displaying his personal possessions, cars and gifts from foreign dignitaries. You must be respectful at all times. It is not advisable to point out that the building housing his tomb resembles the Acropolis in Athens! Visiting the Anit Kabir will take a couple of hours.

Other sites in Ankara include the **Citadel** in the old city, the nearby Roman ruins and the **Museum of Anatolian Civilisations**. The last has an extensive collection of artefacts and should be visited by anyone with an interest in the region's past.

If you have two or more days to spare (say a weekend) then Ankara is a good place from which to visit the region of Cappadocia, south-east of the city. This is a 'must see' site for visitors to Turkey and business executives, who can spare the time, should endeavour to visit the area. It is a three hour drive from Ankara and travel agencies in Ankara can arrange excursions. You can also fly to Neveşehir, one of the two main towns in the region – the other is Ürgüp. The area contains unique and strange natural rock formations known as 'fairy chimneys' and was a centre of Christianity. The region contains many churches and even whole cities carved out of the hillside and underground. Many of the churches are decorated with frescoes and provide a fascinating glimpse of early Christianity in a breathtaking natural setting.

In Ankara, the main shopping districts are Kızılay and around Tunalı Hilmi Caddesi. For Turkish Delight visit the market near the citadel.

Useful contacts

Embassies

UK
Şehit Ersan Caddesi 46/A
Çankaya
❑ Tel: +90 312 468 6230; fax: +90 312 468 3214
E-mail: [britembank@superonline.com]

USA
Atatürk Bulvari, 110
Kavaklıdere
❑ Tel: +90 312 468 6110; fax: +90 312 467 0019
Website: [www.usis-ankara.org.tr/main.htm]

Australia
Nene Hatun Caddesi, 83
06700 Gaziosmanpaşa
❑ Tel: +90 312 446 1180; fax: +90 312 446 1188

Canada
Nene Hatun Caddesi, 75
06700 Gaziosmanpasa
Tel: +90 312 436 1275; fax: +90 312 446 4437

New Zealand
Level 4, Iran Caddesi, 13
Kavaklıdere
❑ Tel: +90 312 467 9054; fax: +90 312 467 9013
E-mail: [newzealand@superonline.com.tr]

İzmir

İzmir is Turkey's third largest city and its largest port. It is the centre of Turkey's extensive maritime sector. The city was virtually destroyed during the War of Independence in 1922-3 and then was rebuilt.

İzmir

Finding your way around İzmir can be confusing at first as the city's main roads radiate out from roundabouts like spokes from a wheel and are criss-crossed by other streets. Many of the streets have numbers rather than names but these do not always follow a logical order and, in addition, some roads have alternative names. The road that runs along the seafront is officially known as Atatürk Caddesi but you will probably hear it referred to only as *Birnici Kordon* (First Cordon). The next road inland is officially Cumhuriyet Caddesi but is better known as *İkinci Kordon* (Second Cordon).

Arrival

Flying is the most convenient method of getting to İzmir from other major Turkish cities such as İstanbul or Ankara; the journey from İstanbul by road takes around eight hours and even longer from Ankara. THY connects İzmir to both these cities and several other centres. Some international airlines also offer services to İzmir although most international flights arriving in the city are charter flights carrying tourists. İzmir is conveniently located for the country's main tourist destinations.

İzmir's Adnan Menderes Airport is located to the north-east of the city. The journey takes around thirty minutes. **Taxi** drivers are reluctant to use their meters on this route and you may have to negotiate a fare into the city centre. The journey should not cost more than the equivalent of US$20–25. You may find it more convenient to arrange to be met.

Accommodation

Hotels

İzmir has several hotels offering business standard service. All are located close to the city centre.

Hilton ★★★★★
Gaziosmanpaşa Bulvari, 7
❑ Tel: +90 232 441 6060; fax: +90 232 441 2277
Website: [www.hilton.com]

The landmark building in the city centre and the best hotel in İzmir.

Grand Hotel Mercure ★★★★★
Cumhuriyet Bulvari, 138
❑ Tel: +90 232 489 4090; fax: +90 232 489 4089
Website: [hotels.wec-net.com.tr/mercure/izmir/ index.html]

This is İzmir's other major, located near the seafront on one of İzmir's two large squares.

Ege Palas ★★★★
Cumhuriyet Caddesi, 210
❑ Tel: +90 232 463 9090; fax: +90 232 463 8100

Located at the northern end of the seafront, this four-star hotel is one of İzmir's newest hotels.

Büyük Efes ★★★★
Gaziosmanpaşa Bulvari, 1
❑ Tel: +90 232 484 4300; fax: +90 232 441 5695

One of the city's oldest hotels which has seen better days. It is still a popular venue for wedding receptions and other functions and can get very busy and noisy.

Mercure Konak ★★★★
Mithatpaşa Caddesi, 128
❑ Tel: +90 232 489 150; fax: +90 232 489 1709

Sister hotel to the Grand Mercure noted above, located in the southern part of the city.

Getting around

Taxi is the most convenient method of getting around but you may have difficulty in finding a reliable driver. The best option is to hail a cab at one of the taxi ranks or from in front of your hotel. You should insist on the use of the meter. No journey in central İzmir should cost more than the equivalent of US$2–3.

Eating and drinking

İzmir, as you would expect, has a wealth of seafood restaurants, especially along the seafront. The best policy is to walk along and choose one that catches your attention. As well as the area around Cumhuriyet Square, Alsancak at the north end of the seafront is a popular eating spot. One of the most popular restaurants with the local business community is the Deniz Restaurant on the ground floor of the İzmir Palas Hotel located on the corner of Atatürk Caddesi and Vasif Cinar Bulvari.

Time off

İzmir's main attraction apart from its location is the city's citadel, known as Kadifekale. This sits on a hill south-east of the city centre and provides spectacular views across İzmir, especially at sunset, which is a popular visiting time. The city's impressive bazaar is to be found in the Konak district.

İzmir's great advantage is that it provides a base from which to visit other places in western Turkey, particularly Ephesus and Pamukkale.

İzmir

Ephesus is one of the best preserved Roman cities in the region, if not the world. It was the site of the **Temple of Diana**, one of the Seven Wonders of the World but no longer in existence. It can be visited in a day from İzmir. The journey takes around an hour and a half by road and it takes about half a day to visit the site. In summer, temperatures are high and the site is very crowded with tour groups. There are also sites of Christian interest in the vicinity, in particular the site where the Virgin Mary supposedly lived out her last days. The spot is now marked by a small chapel.

Pamukkale requires more time as it is a four-hour drive from İzmir. Pamukkale (literally 'cotton castle') gets its name from the spectacular white calcium formations on the hillside formed by mineral deposits from the region's spring waters. The waters are thought to have healing properties and there is a spa at the top of the hill where you can sit in a natural pool filled with Roman columns. The water is warm and slightly fizzy. When in Pamukkale, a visit to Aphrodisias is a must – it is only ten minutes away!

There are also numerous coastal resorts that you can visit from İzmir like Foça, Urla and Çeşme.

Useful contacts

Consulates

USA
Kazim Dirik Caddesi
Atabey İş Merkezi, 13/8
35210 Pasaport
❑ Tel: +90 232 441 2203; fax: +90 232 441 2373

UK
Mahmut Esat Bozkurt Caddesi
1442 Sokak, 49
Alsancak
❑ Tel: +90 232 463 5151; fax: +90 232 421 2914

Airlines

Turkish Airlines
Büyük Efes Hotel
Gaziosmanpaşa Bulvari
❑ Tel: +90 232 425 8280 (reservations)
fax: +90 232 483 6281
British Airways
Sair Esref Bulvari 18/304
Alsancak
❑ Tel: +90 232 441 3829; fax: +90 232 441 6284

Air France
Halıt Ziya Bulvari
1353 Sokak, 1
❑ Tel: +90 232 425 9004

KLM
Adnan Menderes Airport
❑ Tel: +90 232 274 2052

Lufthansa
Adnan Menderes Airport
❑ Tel: +90 232 274 2055

Swissair
Cumhuriyet Square 11/2
❑ Tel: +90 232 421 4757

Adana

Adana is Turkey's fourth largest city and one of its most important industrial centres. The city has enjoyed the benefits of Turkey's recent economic development and experienced great commercial success. This prosperity has been used to expand the city.

The main part of Adana lies on the west bank of the Seyhan Nehri River, with the main commercial district lying at the western end of İnönü Caddesi and south of Turan Cemal Benker Bulvari. This is where the city's main hotels, offices and banks are located.

Arrival

Adana's distance from most of Turkey's other main cities means that flying is the only practical method of reaching the city. THY has daily services to and from İstanbul, İzmir and Ankara. It also offers services to some European cities.

Adana

Adana's **Sakıspaşa Airport** is located just west of the city and the journey into town should take less than fifteen minutes. Taxis are available for the journey and should cost no more than the equivalent of US$6. Taxis drivers are likely to use their meters.

Accommodation

Hotels

Adana does not offer as good a choice of hotels as other major Turkish cities, but does have adequate accomodation for the business traveller.

Seyhan
Turan Cemal Benker Bulvari
❑ Tel: +90 322 457 5810; fax: +90 322 454 2834

This is by far the best hotel in Adana and offers the highest standard of service and facilities.

Büyük Surmeli
Kurtulus Caddesi
❑ Tel: +90 322 352 3600; fax: +90 322 352 1945

Adana Surmeli
İnönü Caddesi
❑ Tel: +90 322 363 3437; fax: +90 322 363 3527
This is a four star sister hotel to the Buyuk Surmeli.

Zaimoğlu
Ozler Caddesi
❑ Tel: +90 322 351 3400; fax: +90 322 351 6811

Also a four-star hotel, the Zaimoğlu is located near the two Surmeli hotels.

Getting around

Adana has a compact city centre and business visitors will be able to walk between most locations. Otherwise, taxis are the best method of getting around the city.

Eating and drinking

Adana does not have a good selection of restaurants outside the hotels listed above. You will however come across plenty of stalls selling the local speciality, Adana Kebab – minced lamb and peppers grilled on a skewer and flavoured with paprika.

One of the most popular restaurants is **Yeni Onbaşılar** on Atatürk Caddesi (tel: +90 322 351 4178); an Adana institution but past its best.

Adana

Time off

Adana's main attractions are its mosques and the Roman bridge across the river at the end of Abdin Paşa Caddesi. The Ulu Mosque on Abdin Paşa Caddesi dates from the sixteenth century and resembles mosques found in Syria and Egypt more than classic Ottoman styles. The impressive **Yağ Mosque** was once the Church of St James. Adana's two main museums, the **Ethnography Museum** and the **Archaeological Museum,** have small but well displayed exhibitions. There is also an **Atatürk Museum** just to the north of the Ulu mosque. The city's covered market is to be found near the famous clock tower.

Useful contacts

US Consulate
Atatürk Caddesi
❑ Tel: +90 322 454 2145; fax: +90 322 457 6591.

Turkish Airlines
Stadyum Caddesi, 32
❑ Tel: +90 322 457 0222; fax: +90 322 454 3088.

9

İskenderun

İskenderun is an ancient town that has become a modern commercial centre. In the 1980s the city, long a major port, grew in importance as the terminus for an oil export pipeline from Iraq. The pipeline closed with Saddam Hussein's August 1990 invasion of Kuwait and the resulting international sanctions against Iraq. Since 1997, with the implementation of the UN oil-for-food programme, limited oil exports have resumed but lack of maintenance and spare parts for the Iraqi sections of the pipeline hamper exports.

Alexander the Great founded the town in 333 BC and its modern name is a Turkish transliteration of its traditional name, Alexandretta. The town's location and port have attracted the attention of numerous conquerors throughout its long history. After the collapse of the Ottoman empire, the town was briefly occupied by the British before becoming a French protectorate. Atatürk reclaimed the town for Turkey in 1938.

The town's main commercial centre is on the waterfront around the square at the end of Sehit Pamir Caddesi.

İskenderun

Here you will find Iskenderun's few hotels, its restaurants, banks and main commercial premises. The main waterfront road is Atatürk Bulvari.

Arrival

İskenderun does not have its own airport. The nearest airports are at Adana and Gaziantep, both of which are a two hour drive away. There is a frequent bus service linking İskenderun with both cities. The bus station is located to the north of the town. Taxis are available for the short drive into the town centre.

Accommodation

İskenderun has a limited range of hotels and none that meet international business standards. The following are some of the better hotels in Iskenderun.

Hotels

Hotel Cabir
Ulucami Caddesi, 16
❑ Tel: +90 326 612 3391; fax: +90 326 612 3393

Grand Hotel Ontur
İnönü Meydani
Dr Muammer Aksoy Caddesi, 8
❑ Tel: +90 326 616 2400; fax: +90 326 616 2410

Arsuz Oteli
Arsuz (Ulucinar)
❑ Tel: +90 326 643 2444; fax: +90 326 643 2448

Getting around

The central commercial area is compact enough to walk around. For longer journeys taxis are available and can be hailed on the street.

Eating and drinking

İskenderun has plenty of inexpensive typical Turkish kebab stalls and restaurants. You will find many in the area between the Hotel Cabir and Sehit Pamir Caddesi. The town's best restaurant is probably the Saray on Atatürk Bulvari.

Time off

Despite Iskenderun's long history, there are almost no sites of historic interest remaining due to the ravages of wars, earthquakes and modern construction. The town's waterfront is its most attractive feature and is a pleasant area for an evening stroll.

Useful contacts

UK Consulate
Consular Agency
Catoni Maritime Agencies
Maresal Çakmak Caddesi, 28
❑ Tel:+90 326 613 0361; fax: +90 326 613 0364.

Antakya

Antakya is an ancient town in the Hatay region which has become an important commercial centre. Business in Antakya is dominated by trade with nearby Arab states such as Syria and Jordan. The town is situated in a fertile plain, making agriculture an important economic activity. In recent years, the area has also developed an industrial base.

As Antioch, the town was an important centre for early Christianity and both St Peter and St Paul are said to have lived there. The church of St Peter, to the north-east of the town, is claimed as the first cathedral and is reputed to be the place where the term Christian was first used.

The Hatay region projects southwards from the Anatolian peninsula along the eastern margin of the Mediterranean. It is the subject of a long-running but dormant dispute between Turkey and Syria. Hatay was part of the Syrian province of the Ottoman empire and was placed under French mandate along with Syria after the First World War. Atatürk subsequently claimed the area and after a brief spell as an independent state it agreed to union with Turkey in 1939. Hatay still has a large Arabic-speaking population and many people speak Turkish only as a second language.

Antakya straddles the banks of the Ası River which was known in ancient times as the Orontes. The main commercial centre is on the west bank around the large Cumhuriyet Alanı. The town's main streets radiate from this point. The main hotels, restaurants, banks and other offices are all found in this vicinity.

Arrival

Antakya does not have an airport; the nearest are at Adana and Gaziantep, both a two-and-a-half-hour bus journey away. There are frequent bus services to Adana,

Gaziantep and İskenderun. The journey to İskenderun takes approximately one hour. The bus station is located on the east bank of the river, near the town centre on the corner of İstikial and Abdurrahman Melek Caddesis. Taxis are available for the short journey into the town centre.

Antakya

Accommodation

Antakya offers a limited range of hotels and none that are of international business standard. The hotels cater primarily for tour groups.

Hotels

Büyük Antakya Oteli
Atatürk Caddesi, 8
❑ Tel: +90 326 213 5860; fax: +90 326 213 5869

This is probably the best hotel in Antakya. It accepts Visa but no other credit card.

Hotel Orontes
İstikial Caddesi, 58
❑ Tel: +90 326 214 5931; fax: +90 326 214 5933

9

Getting around

Taxis can be hailed on the street for journeys around town or further afield. Like many Turkish towns, the main commercial centre is compact and most offices can be reached on foot.

Eating and drinking

As in all Turkish towns, there are numerous inexpensive kebab stalls and restaurants. Many are to be found on İstikal Caddesi near the bus station or on Cumhuriyet Caddesi. Apart from the hotels, the two best restaurants are the Saray and the Han, both on the east bank.

For drinking, there are numerous *birahanes* (literally beer-houses) at the southern end of Hurriyet Caddesi. These are traditionally men-only establishments and women may find the atmosphere unwelcoming.

Time off

Antakya's two main sites of interest are its Archaeological Museum and the church of St Peter. The museum houses a very fine collections of mosaics dating from the first century BC to the fifth century AD. There is also a collection of other Roman artefacts. It is located on the southern side of Cumhuriyet Alani and is open every day except Monday.

Behind the museum along the river bank is the Antakya municipal park, a pleasant area to stroll or to take a break at one of the tea-shops.

The Church of St Peter is located approximately two miles to the north-east of the town. A taxi journey will cost around US$2. The church is open every day except Monday. It is a popular place for local people of all religions to visit on public holidays. Mass is celebrated every Sunday evening. The Capuchin order of monks at the Catholic church in central Antakya (Kurtuluş Caddesi) is responsible for the care of the church and will give further information on services, opening times and its history.

A large bazaar fills the area between the bus station and Kurtuluş Caddesi.

Useful contacts

Turkish Airlines
Ant-tur Antakya Turizm ve Seyahat Acentası
İnönü Caddesi, 150
❑ Tel: +90 326 214 9497; fax: +90 326 214 2712

Bursa

Bursa lies at the heart of one of Turkey's main industrial regions and has expanded greatly in recent years. The city is of historical importance as it is in the traditional homeland of the Ottoman dynasty and was the Ottoman capital before the capture of İstanbul. Bursa has a spectacular setting on the side of the Uludağ mountain with the main streets following the contours of the slope. It is an important spa resort and a popular local tourist destination.

The main commercial district centres on Cumhuriyet Square and Atatürk Caddesi which runs westward towards the Ulu Cami Mosque. Cumhuriyet Square is known locally as *Heykel*, which is the Turkish word for statue and refers to the large equestrian figure of Atatürk in the square. This is the term to use with taxi drivers. There are few business standard hotels in this area and traffic noise makes this an unpleasant part of town in which to stay. The main hotels are located in the northwest suburb of Çekirge, which is a ten minute drive away.

Arrival

Although Bursa has a small airport to the north, it is one of the few major cities that Turkish Airlines does not serve. This may change in the near future with the upgrading of facilities at the airport.

Currently, the most convenient method of travel is by sea and land. From İstanbul, there is a catamaran and bus service. The catamaran goes from İstanbul's Yenikapı Dock to Yalova (north of Bursa on the Sea of Marmara coast) and a frequent bus service connects Yalova and Bursa. For travel in the other direction, you should take a bus that departs at least ninety minutes before the catamaran is scheduled to depart. There are also direct bus services between İstanbul and Bursa. Buses marked *feribotile* are faster as they take the car ferry from Topcular (east of Yalova) rather than completing the whole journey overland. The bus station is located to the north of the city on the road to Yalova. Services to other cities such as Ankara and İzmir also depart from here. The journey to Ankara takes approximately five and a half hours; about six hours to İzmir.

9

Accommodation

Hotels

Çekirge

Hotel Dilmen
I Murat Caddesi
❑ Tel: +90 224 233 9500; fax: +90 224 235 2568

Bursa's top hotel. Although it does not meet the highest international standards, it does provide acceptable facilities and service for business visitors, including its own spa baths and gym. This hotel is not to be confused with the Hotel Dikmen in central Bursa. Ensure that your driver understands the hotel that you require.

Celik Palas
Çekirge
❑ Tel: +90 224 233 3800; fax: +90 224 236 1910

Anatolia
Çekirge Meydanı
❑ Tel: +90 224 233 9400; fax: +90 224 233 9408

Akdoğan
I Murat Caddesi, 1
❑ Tel: +90 224 238 8200; fax: +90 224 236 3129

Büyük Yıldız
Uludağ Yolu, 6
❑ Tel: +90 224 233 9600; fax: +90 224 233 9607

Kervansaray Termal
Çekirge Meydanı
❑ Tel: +90 224 233 9300; fax: +90 224 233 9324

Termal Hotel Gonlu Ferah
I Murat Caddesi, 24
❑ Tel: +90 224 233 9210; fax: +90 224 233 9218

The hotel is classified as three-star and caters for those visiting the spas rather than business executives.

Central Bursa

Safran Oteli
Kale Sokak
❑ Tel: +90 224 224 7216; fax: +90 224 224 7219

Located in a restored Ottoman house west of the city centre opposite the tombs of the Ottoman sultans Osman and Orhan, this is probably the best hotel in central Bursa.

Kervansaray Bursa
Fevzi Cakmak Caddesi, 29
❑ Tel: +90 224 220 0000; fax: +90 224 220 0015

This belongs to the same locally-owned chain as the Kervansaray Termal.

Kent Hotel
Atatürk Caddesi, 69
❑ Tel: +90 224 223 5420; fax: +90 224 224 4015

A three star hotel located on the city's main thoroughfare in the heart of the city's commercial district.

Getting around

Taxis are the most convenient method of getting around and travellers should have few problems hailing one on the street. A journey in central Bursa should cost no more than the equivalent of US$2. The journey from central Bursa to Çekirge should cost no more than the equivalent of US$6. As in other Turkish cities, a higher rate applies for journeys at night.

Eating and drinking

Bursa holds a special place in the culinary as well as political history of Turkey. It was here in the last century

Bursa

that the revolving vertical spit was invented. This device, used for cooking döner kebab, has become the best known feature of Turkish cooking. The inventor was a local chef, İskender (the Turkicised form of Alexander), who also devised a new form of kebab known as İskender or Bursa kebab. Meat carved from the doner is laid on bread, tomato sauce is poured on top and butter is added to finish. In some versions, yoghurt is also poured over the meat and sauce. The other popular local dish is *İnegol koftesi*, named after a nearby village; it is a type of grilled meatball.

You will find numerous kebab stalls serving these local specialities in the Heykal area and along Atatürk Caddesi. Probably the best place for Iskender kebab is the Hacibey Kebapcisi. The restaurant is located on Taşkapı Sokak, off Atatürk Caddesi on the left as you head towards Ulu Cami from Heykel and about halfway between the two. The best place for *Inegol koftesi* is probably the Inegol Koftecisi at 48, Atatürk Caddesi. For tea or coffee, the best café is the Café Koza above Koza Park near the Ulu Cami.

For more formal dining – perhaps to entertain local customers and contacts – all the hotels listed have restaurants. The best in central Bursa is probably the Safran Oteli. Aside from the hotels, the following restaurants offer a high level of service and a good range of food.

Çiçek Izgara
Belediye Caddesi, 15
❑ Tel: +90 224 221 6526

Sezen Restaurant
Çekirge Caddesi, Çekirge
❑ Tel: +90 224 236 9156

Time off

As befits a city with such a rich past, Bursa is full of historical monuments. Most are related to the early years of the Ottoman dynasty. A severe earthquake in 1855 destroyed much of the city including mosques and other historic buildings. However, most were carefully restored and respect the original designs. Those with more than a passing interest in Ottoman history or architecture should obtain a detailed reference.

Bursa

The sites listed here can all be seen in a day but those with less time to spare should at least visit the **Yeşil Mosque** and **Yıldırm Beyazit Mosque** in the east of the city and the markets in the centre.

Ulu Cami: This is probably one of the first buildings you will notice in Bursa as it dominates the western end of Atatürk Caddesi. Although built by the Ottoman sultan Beyazit, it is a classic Seljuk in design with its huge portal, forest of columns inside and mass of domes on the roof. It was completed in 1399 and predates the emergence of a distinctive Ottoman architectural style.

Behind the Ulu Cami is a complex of covered markets and caravanserais. These are still used and provide an opportunity to buy local produce such as silk and a chance to see some picturesque historical buildings. They are the best places to buy local handicrafts such as silk and the Karagoz puppets. Bursa is also famous for its thick towels (supposedly invented for the comfort of those taking the waters). Woollen products are also a local speciality.

The **Koza Han** (behind Koza Park) is the centre of the local silk trade. *Koza* is the Turkish word for silk cocoons, and in June and September the market is full of local villagers selling the harvest of cocoons. The market also sells other goods during the rest of the year. Sandwiched between the Koza Han and Ulu Cami is the **Emir Han**, home of the city's silk brokers. Both *Hans* follow the traditional caravanserai design: two-storeyed buildings surrounding a central courtyard with a fountain. Pack animals were kept in the courtyard, goods were stored in the ground floor rooms and the upper level was where the merchants conducted their business and slept.

Behind the Emir Han is the **Bedestan** or covered market. The market has long spilled outside the confines of the Bedestan and fills the streets surrounding the building.

Bursa's other historic market is located north-east of Heykel; this is the **Bat Pazari** or goose market. It is also known as the ironmonger's market – a more appropriate name as it is dominated by blacksmiths and ironmongers – as well as stalls selling a wide range of goods (but no geese).

Bursa's most famous historic monuments are to the east of the city. These are the Emir Sultan, Yıldırım Beyazit and Yeşil Cami (Green) Mosques.

The **Emir Sultan Mosque** dates from the late Ottoman period. It was largely rebuilt in 1905 and restored in the early 1990s. It is a favourite with pious Muslim residents and visitors. You should ensure that you strictly observe Islamic customs when visiting this mosque.

Yıldırım Beyazit. This mosque was built by the Ottoman sultan Beyazit and the grounds contain his tomb. It was built earlier than the Ulu Cami and was completed in 1391. Beyazit greatly expanded the Ottoman empire before being defeated by Tamerlane and dying in captivity.

The **Yeşil Cami** or the Green Mosque, takes its name from the green-blue tiles that decorate the main prayer room. One of Bursa's most famous monuments, the mosque was built by Beyazit's son Mehmet who succeeded in re-establishing Ottoman's power after the blow inflicted by Tamerlane. Above the mosque entrance is a series of rooms used as living accommodation by Mehmet and his family. There are also rooms where court officials conducted business. In the park stands the Yeşil Turbe, where Mehmet and several family members are buried. Also close by is the Turkish and Islamic Arts Museum.

Bursa's other principal monuments are located in the west of the city, in the area called Hısar. This means fortress in Turkish and is the oldest part of the city. Remnants of the city walls are still visible. In a park above Cemal Nadir Caddesi stand the tombs of Osman and Orhan, the first two Ottoman sultans. The original tombs were destroyed in the 1855 earthquake and the current structures were built by the Sultan Abdul Aziz in 1868 in the baroque style. It is customary to give a small donation to contribute towards the tombs' upkeep.

Bursa's fame as a spa resort makes the city the ideal place to experience a **Turkish bath.** Most of the top hotels in the city and in Çekirge have their own bath facilities. Other baths worth trying include the **Yeni Kaplica** baths on the north-west side of the Kultur Parkı which were substantially rebuilt in the sixteenth century on the site of a Byzantine-era bathing complex. In Çekirge, the Eski Kaplica next to the Kervanseray Termal Hotel, is one of the most attractive bath houses in the city. In the city centre is the less grand Çakır Ağa Hamami, located on the corner of Atatürk and Kazim Baykal Caddesi.

Useful contacts

Tourist office
Atatürk Caddesi at the northern entrance of the Orhan Gazi underpass facing the Koza Han.
❑ Tel: +90 224 251 1834; fax: +90 224 220 1848

Turkish Airlines
Hasim Iscan Caddesi
Tuğla İş Merkezi, 12/E
❑ Tel: +90 224 221 11 67; fax: +90 224 222 18 66

Antalya

Antalya is the largest city on Turkey's central Mediterranean coast and in recent years has become an important tourist centre. Agriculture, light industry and shipping are also important for the local economy. The city's transport links have improved with the opening of a new airport to the east of the city centre. Antalya also boasts good facilities for business travellers.

Visitors flock to Antalya for its beaches and its historic sites. Founded in the first century BC, the city has monuments representing most of the important eras of Turkish history including Roman, Seljuk and Ottoman. The Roman harbour has been restored and is now used as a yacht marina. After the fall of the Ottoman empire, the city was briefly occupied by Italy before being recaptured by Atatürk's forces.

The marina lies at the heart of the modern city centre and the main commercial district. This area is bounded by Cumhuriyet Caddesi and Meydanı to the north and Atatürk Caddesi to the east. In this area you will find most of the city's hotels, restaurants, government offices, banks and business premises.

Arrival

Flying is the most convenient method of travelling to Antalya from other Turkish cities. There are also some direct flights to European cities. Turkish Airlines offers eight daily flights from İstanbul, a twice-daily service from Ankara and direct services to Tel Aviv and Zurich. İstanbul Airlines also offers a daily service to İstanbul and has weekly flights to several European cities. These services cater mainly for tourists.

The airport is located six miles east of the city. Taxis are available for the journey to the city centre and the fare should be no more than US$8. There is also a bus service connecting the airport with the Turkish Airlines office in the city centre. It makes around nine journeys into the city on a daily basis.

Antalya

Accommodation

Antalya possesses a good range of accomodation including international business class hotels. During late September and well into October, finding a room in the city can be difficult due to two popular events held at this time: the Golden Orange Film Festival, immediately followed by the Mediterranean Song Festival.

Hotels

Sheraton Voyager Hotel ★★★★★
100 Yıl Bulvari
❑ Tel: +90 242 243 2432; fax: +90 242 243 2462

This is probably Antalya's best hotel and has all the facilities that you would expect from a hotel in the Sheraton chain. It is located 1.5 miles west of the city centre.

Talya Hotel ★★★★★
Fevzi Çakmak Caddesi, 30
❑ Tel: +90 242 248 6800; fax: +90 242 241 5400

A locally-owned five-star-hotel located just south of the city centre.

Hotel Aspen ★★★★
Mermerli Sokak, 16-18
❑ Tel: +90 242 247 0590; fax: +90 242 241 3364

This is a four star hotel in the city centre, a couple of blocks from the marina. The facilities are excellent.

Getting around

Although the city centre is compact, its maze of streets is confusing. Outside the centre, many offices and hotels are strung out along long boulevards. Taxis are therefore the most convenient method of getting around Antalya and can easily be hailed on the streets. In tourist areas of the city, there is a higher risk of taxi drivers attempting to fiddle the fare. Ensure the meter is used and at the right rate. A long journey within the city should come to no more than US$3.

Eating and drinking

There are numerous restaurants in the city centre clustered around the marina and in the surrounding area. Most cater for the tourist trade and attempt to charge as much as possible for as little food as possible. In general, the closer to the marina, the more expensive the restaurant and the less reliable the quality of food and service. Given the large number of restaurants, it is only possible to provide a small selection here. Ask local contacts for further recommendations.

Şehir Ocakbaşı Restaurant
Cumhuriyet Caddesi
❑ Tel: +90 242 241 5127
(north-east corner of Cumhuriyet Meydanı)

This is one of the best restaurants in the city centre and has a reputation as the place to discuss serious business.

Hisar Restaurant
Cumhuriyet Meydanı
❑ Tel: +90 242 241 5281
(across from the Şehir Ocakbaşı)

This restaurant is better known for its spectacular views across the city and the marina than for its food.

Time off

Despite Antalya's long history, there are few historic sites surviving in the city itself. However, for those with some spare time the city is a good base for exploring nearby sites. Most of the trips take at least half a day and some longer. There are numerous companies offering boat excursions along the coast starting from the marina. These trips typically last around five hours. The price can vary considerably, depending on what the excursion involves and your bargaining powers. Most will include lunch but ask in detail about the type of meal when comparing prices.

Among the sites than can be visited from Antalya are the ruins at **Termessos, Perge, Olimpos, Phaselis, Aspendos** and **Side** dating from Hellenistic and Roman times. Tour agencies in Antalya can arrange half day or full day tours. There are also natural wonders such as the waterfalls at Düden.

In Antalya itself, the main monuments include the restored Roman harbour used as the yacht marina, **Hadrian's Gate**,

Antalya

some Seljuk remains and the city museum. Hadrian's Gate is located on Atatürk Caddesi and is a triumphal arch built to mark the Emperor Hadrian's visit to the city in AD 130. The chief Seljuk monument is the **Yivli** (grooved) minaret on Cumhuriyet Caddesi just east of Cumhuriyet Square. The minaret was built in the early thirteenth century when the church on the site was converted to a mosque by the Seljuk sultan and stands across from the bazaar. The Kesik minaret in the eastern part of the old city was similarly added to a church on its conversion to a mosque. The minaret is all that is left of what was once a substantial building.

Antalya Museum is west of the city centre close to the Sheraton Hotel. It has a fine collection of artefacts from Turkish history including a collection of Christian icons and relics. One of these is supposedly the jawbone of St Nicholas, who lived in Anatolia and is the basis for Santa Claus.

Useful Contacts

Airlines

Turkish Airlines
Cumhuriyet Caddesi, 91
❑ Tel: +90 242 243 4383; fax: +90 242 248 4761

İstanbul Airlines
Güllük Caddesi, 2
Selekler Çarşısı 82
❑ Tel: + 90 242 243 3890; fax: +90 242 3894

Consulates

UK
Kızılsaray Mahallesi
Dolaplıdere Caddesi
Pırıltı Sitesi, Kat 1
Ilit Sauna Karsisi
❑ Tel: +90 242 247 7000; fax: +90 242 247 7005

Germany
Atatürk Caddesi, 9/9
❑ Tel: +90 242 241 3318

Italy
İsiklar Caddesi
1321 Sokak, 3
❑ Tel: +90 242 248 5090

Antalya

Spain
Konyaaltı Caddesi
Sitki Goksoy Apt 40/2
❑ Tel: +90 242 241 7770

Sweden
Konyaaltı Bulvari, 78
❑ Tel: +90 242 248 9060; fax: +90 242 241 5222

Turkish Republic of Northern Cyprus
Kisla Mahallesi
35 Sokak, Dortelddemir Apt 11
❑ Tel: +90 242 248 9847

Gaziantep

Gaziantep is Turkey's sixth largest city with a population of 650,000 and the main economic centre of the south-east. The city has been one of the main beneficiaries of the conflict in the south-east, since it has served as a safe haven outside the conflict zone for those fleeing the fighting further east. Gaziantep has also taken advantage of the rich agricultural land around it to build its prosperity; industries based on agricultural produce such as cotton processing, food processing and packaging and textile production are the mainstay of the local economy.

The city's main business district is centred on the crossroads where the city's four main arteries meet. These are Atatürk Bulvari to the west, Suburcu Caddesi to the east, İstasyon Caddesi to the north and Hürriyet Caddesi to the south. Most of the main commercial premises, hotels and government offices are located on Atatürk Bulvari and Suburcu Caddesi near this intersection or in blocks south of here.

During the Ottoman era, the town was known as Aintab. It gained the title 'Gazi' and the name was Turkicised to its current form in honour of the bravery of its population during the War of Independence. During the war, in 1920, the city's inhabitants resisted French attempts to seize the area and add it to her mandated territories in Lebanon and Syria. The city held out for ten months at considerable loss of life. This stalwart resistance came to be seen as one of the defining moments of the war and a key episode in the creation of the new republic.

Gaziantep

Arrival

Gaziantep's distance from other major Turkish business centres means that air travel is the most convenient method of reaching the city. Turkish Airlines (THY) operates daily flights to Gaziantep from both İstanbul (flight time one hour and forty five minutes) and Ankara (flight time one hour). İstanbul Airlines also operates a regular service to the city. Gaziantep's Oğzeli airport is south-east of the city centre with taxis readily available for the journey into the city centre.

Hotels

Accommodation

Gaziantep has a limited range of business class hotels but the city's rapid expansion may lead to a greater range of hotels in the future. The few hotels that are available are located in the city's main business district.

***Tuğcan Oteli* ★★★★**
Atatürk Bulvari
❑ Tel: +90 342 220 4323, fax: +90 342 220 3242.

Undoubtedly the city's best hotel.

***Sevcan Oteli* ★★★★**
One block west of Hürriyet Caddesi on Güzelce Sokak
❑ Tel: +90 342 220 6686, fax: +90 342 220 8237.

This is one of the newest hotels in the city.

Other hotels suitable for business executives include:

Tilmen Oteli
Alaybey Mahallesi, İnönü Caddesi, 168
❑ Tel: +90 342 220 2081; fax: +90 342 220 2091

Yesemek Oteli
İsmail Say Sokak, 4 Suburcu Caddesi
❑ Tel: +90 342 220 9581; fax: +90 342 220 8888

Gap Oteli
Atatürk Bulvari, 10
❑ Tel: +90 342 220 3974; fax: +90 342 220 2102

The *Büyük Velic*, the *Güllüoğlu* and *Büyük Murat* hotels are not recommended as they suffer from high levels of noise, especially from traffic.

Getting around

The business district is very compact and can be easily walked around. Taxis can be used for visits to more outlying areas. You are likely to find that visits to outlying premises such as factories are arranged by local contacts.

Eating and drinking

Gaziantep's location in an agricultural area has allowed it to gain a reputation for its food. In particular, Gaziantep is famous for its baklava (sweet pastries), especially those containing pistachios (*fistıklı*). The area is also well known for its fruit and for a savoury pastry similar to a pizza called a *lahmacun*.

There are scores of cafés, pastry shops and restaurants along Atatürk Bulvari and Suburcu Caddesi where you can sample these local specialities and the full range of Turkish cuisine. The Güllüoğlu hotel on Suburcu Caddesi has one of the most famous cafés. This makes a good place to take a break if not to stay during your visit. Other good patisseries include Cicim on Atatürk Bulvari and the nearby Liman and Kenem cafés.

Probably the best place to go for a meal and to entertain local contacts is the rooftop restaurant at Kaleli Oteli. There are also numerous restaurants in the shopping complex on the corner of Suburcu and Hürriyet Caddesi, the best of these being the Altınkupa.

Time off

Despite Gaziantep's long history, there are few sites of historic interest remaining. It does however possess a few good museums. The main historic site that dominates the city's skyline is the citadel (*kale*). Access to this is limited however and you are unlikely to be able to gain entry to the fortified enclosure. The original citadel was built in the time of the Byzantine emperor Justinian but the surviving building dates largely from the Seljuk era in the twelth and thirteenth centuries. At the foot of the citadel is a traditional bazaar with a wide range of stalls serving foodstuffs and local crafts.

Several well preserved examples of historic mosques and houses can be found in the area immediately to the south of Atatürk Bulvari and to the west of Hürriyet Caddesi. This area also contains the city's **Ethnography Museum** which is located in a traditional Gaziantep stone house and details traditional life in the city.

The **Archaeological Museum** at the northern end of İstasyon Caddesi provides a well displayed and thorough explanation of the area's history from earlier times. The Museum is closed on Mondays.

As befits Gaziantep's prominent role in the War of Independence, there are several monuments to one of the most glorious moments in the city's history. The Ethnography Museum has a room dedicated to the War. There is a war monument on Atatürk and a War museum on Belediye Caddesi, south-east of the city centre.

Useful contacts

Airlines

Turkish Airlines
Atatürk Bulvari, 30/B
❑ Tel: +90 342 230 1565; fax: +90 342 230 1567

İstanbul Airlines
Atatürk Bulvari, 63
❑ Tel: +90 342 230 0048; fax: +90 342 230 7866

Business organisations

Chamber of Trade
❑ Tel: +90 342 220 3030

Chamber of Commerce
❑ Tel: +90 342 233 3957

Hospitals

Devlet Hastanesi
Hürriyet Caddesi
❑ Tel: +90 342 220 9339

Gaziantep Üniversitesi Tip Fakültesi Hastanesi
Ali Fuat Cebesoy Bulvari
❑ Tel: +90 342 336 5400

Mersin

Mersin's official name was recently changed to İcel to coincide with the name of the province of which it is the capital. The name has never really stuck and the vast majority of people still use Mersin. It is one of Turkey's major ports and is certainly the most important port on the south Aegean coast. The city was built in the post-Second World War period as a port for Adana (40 miles to the east) and for the export of agricultural produce. The city has grown rapidly and now has a population of around 1.5 million.

The city's business district is centred on **Gümrük Meydanı,** which is just behind the waterfront Atatürk Park. The port is close by to the east. To the north of the square is İstikal, the city's main street and to the west is the pedestrianised Atatürk Caddesi, which forms the main shopping district. İsmet İnönü Caddesi runs eastward to the port and beyond that to the Hilton Hotel.

Arrival

Mersin has no airport of its own; the nearest is at Adana. The two cities are connected by a good quality four-lane highway and there are frequent bus services. Mersin's bus station is located on the eastern outskirts of the city. Taxis are available for the journey into the city centre.

Accommodation

As befits a city of Mersin's commercial importance, it has a good range of business standard hotels. Business travellers, especially women, should be wary of staying at Mersin's less expensive hotels. Many have reputations as meeting places for prostitutes and their clients.

9

Hotels

Hilton Hotel
Adnan Menderes Bulvari
❑ Tel: +90 324 326 5000; fax: +90 324 326 5050

This has all the facilities and the high standards of service you would expect from this international chain.

Merit Hotel
Kuvayi Milliye Caddesi, 165
❑ Tel: +90 324 336 1010; fax: +90 324 336 0722

The city's tallest building and therefore something of a local landmark, the Merit is located just north of Gümrük Meydanı.

Mersin Oteli
Gümrük Meydanı
❑ Tel: +90 324 238 1040; fax: +90 324 231 2625

A four-star hotel on the waterfront.

Getting around

The pedestrianised areas in central Mersin make the city one of the more pedestrian-friendly cities in Turkey; many places in the central business area can be easily reached on foot. For longer journeys, taxis are readily available and fares should not exceed the equivalent of US$3.

Mersin

Eating and drinking

As you would expect in a coastal city, Mersin was several good fish restaurants. These are mainly found on Soğuksu Caddesi, which runs north-west from Gümrük Meydanı. One of the best is the Agora. At the Gümrük Meydanı end of this street is another recommended restaurant, the Kervan. If you just want to take a break for tea or coffee, try the Denizkızı Patisserie on Ismet İnönü Caddesi.

Time off

As Mersin is a modern city there are virtually no sites of historic interest. The city does have a small museum housing a collection of Roman artefacts, and Mersin's waterfront and the Atatürk Park are pleasant areas for a walk on Atatürk Caddesi. However, it is possible to visit Tarsus, the birthplace of St Paul, to the east on the Adana road.

Useful Contacts

Consulates

UK Vice-Consulate
Catoni Maritime Agencies
Çakmak Caddesi
Mersin Orta Okulu Sokak 3/B
❑ Tel: +90 324 232 1248; fax: +90 324 232 2991

Samsun

Samsun is the largest city and port on the Black Sea coast (in population terms) and is therefore an important commercial centre. The surrounding area is a rich agricultural region with crops growing on the rich deposits of the Kızılırmak and Yeşilirmak rivers. The city has a long history as shown by the artefacts dating from the Bronze age displayed in the city's Archaeological Museum. Little of ancient Samsun has survived as the Genoese burnt the city to the ground in the fifteenth century. Samsun played an important role in the War of Independence following the collapse of the Ottoman empire; it was here that Atatürk rallied the Turkish forces against the occupying European powers. This is commemorated in the city's Atatürk Museum.

Samsun

Samsun's main business district is centred on **Cumhuriyet Meydanı**, one block from the seafront. The main business thoroughfare is Kazim Paşa Caddesi (also known as Bankalar Caddesi), which heads westward from the square. In this area are the city's main business and government offices, banks, hotels and restaurants. The city's bazaar is to the south of Kasim Paşa Caddesi.

Arrival

Samsun's distance from other major Turkish cities means that flying is the most convenient method of reaching the city. Turkish Airlines offers daily direct services from İstanbul. Samsun's Carsamba Airport is located sixteen miles east of the city and visitors should allow around forty minutes for the journey to or from the airport. Taxis are available.

Accommodation

Samsun has an adequate range of hotels including one five-star hotel and several others of suitable for business travellers. All are located in the central business district.

Büyük Samsun Oteli
Sahil Caddesi, 629
❑ Tel: +90 362 435 4999; fax: +90 362 431 0740

Samsun's top hotel, located on the waterfront, north-west of Cumhuriyet Meydanı. It has recently been completely refurbished.

Vidinli Oteli
Kazim Paşa Caddesi
❑ Tel: +90 362 431 6050; fax: +90 362 431 2136

Hotels

Hotel Yafeya
Cumhuriyet Meydanı
❑ Tel: +90 362 435 1131; fax: +90 362 435 1135

Location makes traffic noise a problem in most of the rooms.

Getting around

Taxis fares should come to no more than the equivalent of US$2. Many trips in the central business area can be accomplished on foot.

Eating and drinking

Samsun city centre has many typical Turkish kebab restaurants but also a good range of other restaurants and cafés. Among the recommended restaurants are Sila on Irmak Caddesi (east of the square) and on Osmaniye Caddesi (south of the square) are Oba and Ovalı. For a coffee break and a pastry, try the Birtat and Divan cafés; both are on Irmak Caddesi.

Time off

For those with a little time to spare, the only places of interest in Samsun are the Archaeological Museum and the Atatürk Museum. They are next to each other on Fuar Caddesi near the waterfront and the Büyük Samsun Hotel.

Useful Contacts

Turkish Airlines
Kazim Paşa Caddesi, 18
❑ Tel: +90 362 435 2330; fax: +90 362 431 8260

Trabzon

Trabzon's location at the eastern end of Turkey's Black Sea coast makes the city an important trading centre. Trabzon is Turkey's largest Black Sea port (in terms of traffic handled) and it has become an important centre for trade with Georgia, Armenia and other former Soviet Union republics. Although this has brought prosperity to the town, it has also led to an influx of prostitutes – known locally as Natashas – and other unsavoury characters.

Trabzon is a compact city and business travellers will find most facilities within a small area. The main commercial district is centred on Atatürk Square, which is just to the west of the main port and a few blocks from the seafront. Around Atatürk Square you will also find most government offices, exchange facilities, airline offices, the main hotels and a wide selection of restaurants. The city's transport links also converge on the square.

Arrival

Trabzon's distance from other Turkish cities means that flying is the only practical method of reaching the city. Turkish Airlines has several daily flights to Trabzon from both İstanbul and Ankara. İstanbul Airlines also has a frequent service to the city. Trabzon's airport is located east of the city and the journey into the centre takes approximately twenty

Trabzon

minutes. Taxis are available for the journey or there is a bus service, which takes passengers to the THY office in Atatürk Square. The bus journey costs the equivalent of US$1 and the taxi journey around US$4.

Accommodation

Trabzon's range of business standard hotels is limited. Most are favourite hang-outs for the Natashas and foreign women business travellers may find the atmosphere at some hotels intimidating, especially if they are travelling alone. Smartly dressed foreign women risk being mistaken for prostitutes and may receive unwelcome attention. While it is possible for foreign women to travel to Trabzon on their own and successfully conduct business, they should be aware that the trip is likely to be more challenging than travel to most other Turkish cities.

9

Hotels

Grand Hotel Zorlu
Maraş Caddesi, 9
❑ Tel: +90 462 326 8400; fax: +90 462 326 8458

Trabzon's only five-star hotel is located one block west of Atatürk Square. It is a modern hotel, with all the facilities that business travellers require.

Hotel Usfa
Telgrafhane Sokak, 1
❑ Tel: +90 462 326 5700; fax: +90 462 322 3793

Trabzon's only other business class hotel has four stars and is located on the north-east corner of Atatürk Square.

Getting around

Most points in central Trabzon, are easily reached on foot except in the summer months when the heat can be oppressive. At night, the increased risk of petty crime makes it advisable to take taxis. These are also the most convenient option for longer journeys. They can be hailed on the street and most journeys should cost no more than the equivalent of US$2.

Eating and drinking

Trabzon has a good selection of typical Turkish restaurants, many of which can be found in the Atatürk Square area. Again, women business travellers may find some of these places intimidating, especially at night, when they tend to be male-dominated. There are few formal places to eat outside the main hotels. Many of the

Trabzon

menus in Trabzon's restaurants have a distinctly Russian flavour to cater for the large number of Russian visitors.

Time off

For those with some spare time, Trabzon has an impressive array of Byzantine monuments to visit. The Byzantine imperial clan and other leading families sought sanctuary in the city when soldiers of the Fourth Crusade occupied Constantinople in 1204. A separate Byzantine empire was established in the region and survived until the Ottomans captured the city in 1461. Trabzon continued to have a large Greek population until the collapse of the Ottoman empire when attempts were made to create a separate Greek state in the region. Most Greeks left in the population exchange of the 1920s.

The city's most famous site, the **Sumela Monastery**, is located in the hills to the south of the city. A trip to the site takes the best part of a day, although a visit can be fitted into a morning if organised privately. By leaving early in the morning and returning before lunch, you will miss the crowds and have a better chance of seeing the monastery at its best. The road journey to Sumela takes about forty-five minutes and then there is a steep climb on foot of about an hour to reach the site. When the monastery is not covered in mist (as it is most of the time) there are impressive views. The monastery is now ruined but a considerable amount of decoration remains. The Ulusoy bus company runs a daily service to the foot of the hill, leaving in the morning and returning mid afternoon. Tour companies in Trabzon also offer organised trips taking a similar time. There are restaurants at the foot of the hill. the

Trabzon's other main Byzantine monument is the church of **Aya Sofya**, to the west of the city. The journey takes about ten minutes in a taxi. The church is now a museum and is closed on Mondays. Although not as grand as its namesake in İstanbul, it has impressive Byzantine frescoes and mosaics. On the way to Aya Sofya, you will pass the remains of the city walls towering above a ravine. The walls are quite extensive and enclose an area of narrow streets and parks, with spectacular views across the city.

The main bazaar is just to the north-west of Atatürk Square, along Kunduracilar Sokak which is off Gazipaşa Caddesi (the road that runs north-south along the western

Trabzon

edge of the square). The bazaar contains a traditional *han* of shops and workshops set around a courtyard. On the edge of Trabzon you will come across many open air markets where citizens of the former Soviet Union sell goods out of the boots of their cars. One of the biggest is east of Atatürk Square on the road to the airport.

Useful Contacts

Airlines

Turkish Airlines
Atatürk Alanı (south-west corner of the square)
❑ Tel: +90 462 321 1680

İstanbul Airlines
Atatürk Alanı (north-west corner of the square)
❑ Tel: +90 462 321 1367

Consulates

Georgia and Russia are the only countries that maintain consulates in the city. The Georgian consulate issues visas to third country nationals. The Russian consulate does not.

Georgian Consulate
Gazipaşa Caddesi, 20
❑ Tel: +90 462 326 2226; fax: +90 462 326 2296

9

Diyarbakır

Diyarbakır is the largest city in the troubled south-east of Turkey. It is therefore an important regional base for business in the area, especially Turkey's oil exploration industry and the massive South-East Anatolian Project, known by its Turkish initials GAP. This project involves the construction of a series of dams in the region to produce hydro-electricity for local industry and to increase the amount of agricultural land. GAP should make a significant contribution to the economic development of a region blighted by years of guerrilla insurgency.

The level of violence has decreased markedly since the start of 1999 and the number of visitors (both business and tourist) is slowly increasing. The city is developing the infrastructure to deal with increased visitor numbers. Despite the easing of tensions in the south-east, Diyarbakır's reputation for violence persists and you may find the atmosphere in the city intimidating. Levels of violent crime are higher here than in other Turkish cities and it is unwise to wander around the town after dark, especially on your own.

The central part of Diyarbakır is surrounded by ancient walls and is oriented towards the points of the compass. Major north-south and east-west roads bisect the city and join the four main city gates Dağ (north), Mardin (south), Yeni (east) and Urfa or Edessa west. This outline follows the original Roman layout of the city. The main commercial centre is at the north gate in the area bounded by İnönü Caddesi to the south. The city has grown rapidly in recent years and has spilled out of the city walls. This growth is due mainly to villagers fleeing the troubles in the countryside.

Arrival

Diyarbakır's distance from other major Turkish business centres means that flying is the only practical means of getting to and from the city. Turkish Airlines operates daily direct flights from Ankara, İstanbul and İzmir to the city's Kaplaner Airport, located to the west of the city. Taxis are available for the journey to the city centre and should cost around US$4. There is also a bus service, which departs three times a day and drops passengers at the Turistik Hotel in the city centre.

Accommodation

The choice of hotels in Diyarbakır remains limited despite attempts to improve the facilities for business visitors.

***Dedeman Hotel* ★★★★★**
❑ Tel: +90 800 211 4444.

Just north of Dağ Kapısı next to the Archaeological Museum

This hotel is operated by a Turkish-owned chain and offers all the facilities you would expect.

***Turistik Oteli* ★★★**
Ziya Gökalp Bulvari, 7
❑ Tel: +90 412 224 7550; fax: +90 412 224 4274

Located one block south of the Dedeman and, prior to that hotel's construction, probably the best hotel in Diyarbakır.

Diyarbak›r

Demir Otel ★★★★
Izzet Paşa Caddesi, 8
❑ Tel: +90 412 228 8800; fax: +90 412 228 8809

Located within the city walls near Dağ Kapisi and popular with tour groups.

Getting around

The commercial centre of the city is small enough to walk around. For longer trips and for journeys at night, taxis are readily available.

Eating and drinking

Diyarbakır has more than its fair share of inexpensive kebab stalls and restaurants. There is a wide variety on Kıbrıs Caddesi, which runs westward from Dağ Kapisi. Very few restaurants in the city serve alcohol. The main exceptions are the hotel restaurants and the Sinan Lokantasi, near the Dağ Kapisi.

Time off

For those with some spare time and a desire to explore more of the walled city, a guide is advisable as it is very easy to get lost in the maze of narrow streets. Your hotel or a local travel agent will be able to arrange a reliable guide. Diyarbakır's star attraction is undoubtedly the city walls. It is possible to walk along the walls and visit the gates. Again a guide or an organised tour is recommended as lone visitors face an increased risk of robbery.

Diyarbakır's other sites include the **Archaeological Museum** and the **Atatürk Köskü** (also known as the Seman Kosku). This villa is located to the south of the city centre and is one of the best preserved examples of a traditional Diyarbakır house.

Contact

Turkish Airlines
İnönü Caddesi, 8
❑ Tel: +90 412 221 2314; fax: +90 412 224 3366

This section gives general information and advice on what to do in the evening and activities such as shopping and sports. If you have some spare time for sightseeing or relaxation you should refer to the Time Off sections in the city listings in Chapter 9.

10

a break from business

10

a break from business

It would be a crime to come to Turkey on business and to ignore the spectacular historic sites, impressive scenery, good beaches and the opportunities for cultural and sporting activities. Turkey is an ideal country to add a few day's leave to the end of your trip or to return to for a longer holiday with a well-developed tourist infrastructure and numerous travel agencies which can arrange tailor-made excursions and tours.

What to do in the Evenings

Night life

You will find that the streets really come alive at night, especially in the spring and summer. Squares, popular commercial streets and malls will be crowded with people. Shops stay open late, and cafés and bars are full of people unwinding and wanting to see and be seen. Restaurants start to fill up as eating out is a popular leisure activity. Evening meals start quite late, from 9 p.m. onwards.

Most Turkish cities have a lively nightlife with numerous bars and nightclubs. Bars in the top hotels and some other nightclubs stage regular 'traditional' Turkish bellydancing shows. Business visitors should stick to reputable venues and go only with known local contacts. Be wary of casual acquaintances attempting to persuade you to visit a particular venue; it may be the prelude to one of the scams noted in *Watch out!* (Chapter 4) or you may just get ripped off. Women executives should be cautious about visiting bars and nightclubs on their own or even in all-women groups. At best you will attract a lot of unwelcome attention at worst you may be mistaken for prostitutes and receive sexual attention.

Cinema

If you want a more cultural evening, cinema and theatre-going are popular and you may be able to find a film or show in English or another European language. You will find recent US and British films on release in the cinemas. Before you buy a ticket, check whether the film has been dubbed into Turkish or whether subtitles have been added. Theatre productions will invariably be in Turkish but foreign companies do tour and foreign cultural institutions such as the British Council arrange shows. Look in the Turkish Daily News for listings or contact the organisations direct. (See below.) There are also frequent orchestral and other music performances.

A Turkish Bath

Turkish Bath

If you really want to relax after a hard day's work, then take a Turkish bath (known locally as a *hammam*). There are baths for men and women, but never mixed bathing. After undressing in a cubicle and donning a towel you go into the steam room where you can just sit and relax or wash yourself down. You can also get a massage from one of the attendants. Be warned; these are not gentle affairs. You will be pummelled and stretched in all directions. At the end you will feel that all the stress has been hammered out of you. It feels great! You pay on leaving. It is normal to tip the attendants. In İstanbul, the **Çagaloğlu** and **Galatasaray** are recommended, but ask for local recommendations for reputable bath-houses.

Shopping

10

For many, Turkey conjures up images of crowded bazaars and haggling over the price of carpets, jewellery and other artefacts. This does still exist to an extent. The reality, however, is a wide range of shops with familiar names selling familiar goods at prices lower than in the UK and Western Europe. Credit cards are widely accepted, especially Visa and Mastercard but not American Express. Shops tend to stay open late into the evening but close on Sunday and public holidays.

Prices may be generally lower than you would pay at home but beware; you may not be buying what you think. Counterfeiting of goods, especially music tapes, CDs and computer software, is rife. Perfumes and designer clothes labels are also popular targets for counterfeiters. If you buy the goods in the company's store or in another reputable shop then you are probably getting the genuine item. In smaller independent shops, you may be getting a fake.

Counterfeit goods

Carpets

At some point on your visit, you will be invited to buy a carpet or at least have a look. This is especially true in tourist areas. If you take a look, accept the offer of free tea or a soft drink but do realise that when the vendor names a price, you are under no obligation to accept. You can look at as many carpets and drink as much tea as you want. However, if you make a counter offer, this may be accepted as an intention to buy and serious haggling will ensue. You may then find it difficult to escape. Buying a carpet can be a lengthy business and it is best not left to your last afternoon in the country. It will probably require several visits to the dealer and a lengthy negotiating process. It is best to go to a dealer recommended by a local contact; there is less chance of being conned. After you have bought the carpet, decide whether you would prefer the dealer to ship it home or take it yourself. There have been reports of buyers receiving an inferior carpet to the one they bought after arranging for the dealer to ship it but such incidents are rare. Ensure you keep all receipts and if necessary obtain a certificate from the dealer that the carpet is not antique. There are harsh penalties for exporting antiques of any kind.

Other local products

Leather. Check all items carefully for quality of workmanship and flaws. A huge range of goods is available including jackets, bags, wallets and shoes.

Meerschaum. This is a white mineral that is only mined in Turkey and is made into pipes for smoking and other items. Again carefully check items for flaws and quality. The bowl of the pipe and the underneath should be smooth. Any small carved designs in these places are intended to hide flaws. If the pipe is used for smoking, it will turn brown over time.

Wood. You will see chess and backgammon sets, boxes and tables decorated with inlaid woods and mother-of pearl everywhere. Check for authenticity. These days the pattern can be replicated on transfers stuck on to plain wood.

Spices and sweets. Turkey is famous for its Turkish Delight (known locally as *lokum*) and you will see it sold everywhere. In confectioners, it is fine to ask for a sample to taste before buying. Fresh Turkish Delight should melt in the mouth. The chewier it is, the older it is. If you are taking it back as a present, buy at the last minute. You will also come across shops and market stalls selling a wide variety of spices, nuts and other foodstuffs. Adana has its own covered market near the city's famous clock tower.

Sports

Turks are mad about sport, especially football (soccer). You will know when there is a match on by the number of people in their team's colours. After the match, fans take to the streets and make a great deal of noise. Turkish soccer fans have a reputation for violence (especially in the British press) following clashes between Turkish fans and visiting English fans. However, violence is rare at domestic matches. Trouble is more likely to occur during matches between Turkish teams and visiting European teams, especially those from England, the Netherlands, Germany and Greece. You will undoubtedly be asked which team you support (especially if you are male). Due to high tensions with Leeds United and Manchester United fans, you should be careful about which team you claim to support. Turks are very knowledgeable about the top European teams, especially the top English ones.

If you want to participate in sport yourself, there are plenty of opportunities. Many of the hotels listed in this guide have facilities such as gyms, swimming pools, tennis courts and squash courts. If you want to go running, remember that both İstanbul and Ankara are very hilly and have poor air quality and poor driving standards. In addition, many pavements are in bad repair. However, some cities possess parks which provide pleasant areas to run, and in coastal towns it may be possible to use the seafront. In İzmir, there is the corniche.

For more adventurous sports and for those with some time to spare, Turkey offers excellent opportunities for sailing and diving. There are numerous travel agencies that will offer these types of activities and some useful contact details are listed below.

Useful contacts

Tourist offices

İstanbul

There are tourist information offices at Atatürk International Airport, at the north-west end of the Hippodrome in Sultanahmet, at the Hilton hotel, and on Mesrutiyet Caddesi, almost opposite the British Consulate.

Ankara

Gazi Mustafa Kemal Bulvari, 121

❑ Tel:+90 312 231 5572

İzmir
There are tourist information offices at the Büyük Efes hotel and at the airport.

Adana
Atatürk Caddesi, 13
❑ Tel: +90 322 359 1994

This is only open on weekdays. There is also an office at the airport.

Cultural institutions

British Council

Website: [www.britcoun.org.tr/index.htm]

İstanbul
Ors Turistik İş Merkezi
İstiklal Caddesi, 251/523, Kat 2-6)
Beyoğlu 80060
❑ Tel: +90 212 252 7474; fax: +90 212 252 8682
E-mail: [bc-istanbul@britcoun.org.tr]

Ankara
Esat Caddesi, 41
Küçükesat, 06660
Ankara
❑ Tel: +90 312 468 6192; fax: +90 312 427 6182
E-mail: [bc.ankara@britcoun.org.tr]

İzmir
İsmet Kaptan Mah.
1374 Sokak,
Selvili İş Merkezi, 18
Kat 3, Daire 301-306
❑ Tel: +90 232 446 0131; fax: +90 232 446 0130
E-mail: [bc-izmir@britcoun.org.tr]

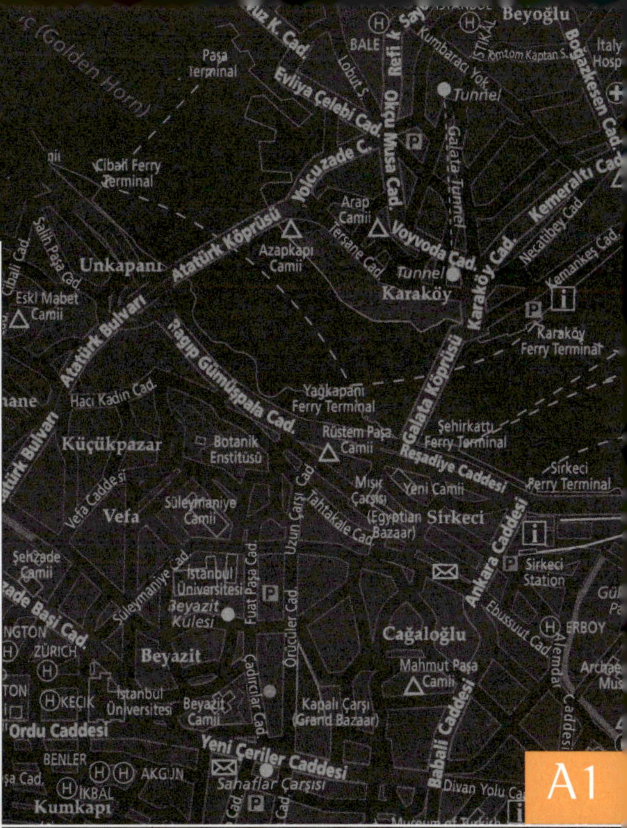

appendix one

appendix one

A1

Emergencies

Ambulance	112
Police	155
Fire	110

Hotels

İstanbul

Hilton ★★★★★
Cumhuriyet Caddesi
t: +90 212 231 4650; ***f:*** +90 212 240 4165
Website: [www.hilton.com]

Hyatt Regency ★★★★★
Taşkışla Caddesi
t: +90 212 225 7000 ***f:*** +90 212 225 7007
Website: [www.hyatt.com]

Ceylan Intercontinental ★★★★★
Taksim Parkı
t: +90 212 231 2121 ***f:*** +90 212 231 2180
Website: [www.interconti.com]

Divan ★★★★★
Cumhuriyet Caddesi
t: +90 212 231 4100 ***f:*** +90 212 248 8257

Marmara ★★★★
Taksim Square
t: +90 212 251 4696 ***f:*** +90 212 244 0509

Pera Palas ★★★★
Meşrutiyet Caddesi
t: +90 212 251 4560 ***f:*** +90 212 251 4089

Richmond ★★★★★
İstiklal Caddesi
t: +90 212 252 5460 ***f:*** +90 212 252 9707

Mercure ★★★★★
Meşrutiyet Caddesi
t: +90 212 251 4646 ***f:*** +90 212 249 8033
Website: [http://hotels.wecnet.com.tr/mercure/istanbul/index]

Çirağan Palace Kempinski ★★★★★
Çirağan Caddesi
t: +90 212 258 3377 **f:** +90 212 259 6687

Conrad International ★★★★★
Yıldız Caddesi, Beşiktaş
t: +90 212 227 3000 **f:** +90 212 259 6667

Swissôtel ★★★★★
Bayildım Caddesi, Maçka, Besiktaş
t: +90 212 259 0101 **f:** +90 212 259 0105
Website: [www.swissotel.com]

Four Seasons ★★★★★
Tevkifhane Sokak
t: +90 212 638 8200 **f:** +90 212 638 8210
Website: [www.fshr.com]

Arcadia ★
Dr Imren Oktem Caddesi
t: +90 212 516 9696 **f:** +90 212 516 6118

Yeşil Ev
Kabasakal Caddesi, 5
t: +90 212 517 6785 **f:** +90 212 517 6780

Mavi Ev (Blue House)
Dalbastı Sokak, 14
t: +90 212 638 9010 **f:** +90 212 638 9017
E-mail: [bluehouse@istanbulhotels.com]

Ayasofya Pansiyonlari
Soğukcesme Sokak
t: +90 212 513 3660 **f:** +90 212 513 3669
E-mail: [ayapans@escortnet.com.tr]

Ankara

Hilton
Tahran Caddesi, 12
t: +90 312 468 2888 **f:** +90 312 468 0909
Website: [www.hilton.com]

Sheraton ★★★★★
Noktalı Sokak
t: +90 312 468 5454 **f:** +90 312 467 1136
Website: [www.sheraton.com]

Best ★★★★
Atatürk Bulvari, 195
t: +90 312 467 0880 **f:** +90 312 467 0885

Tetra Konur
Konur Sokak, 58
t: +90 312 419 2946 **f:** +90 312 417 4915

Hospitals

İstanbul

Alman Hastanesi
Sıraselviler Caddesi, 119
Taksim
t: +90 212 293 2150

American
Guzelbahçe Sokak,20
Nisantasi
t: +90 212 231 4050

Florence Nightingale
Abidei Hürriyet Caddesi, 290
Şişli
t: +90 212 231 2021

Intermed Check-up Centre
Teşvikiye Caddesi
Bayar Apt 143
Nişantaşı
t: +90 212 225 0660

International
İstanbul Caddesi, 82
Yeşilyurt
t: +90 212 663 3000

La Paix Hastanesi
Büyükdere Caddesi, 22-24
Şişli
t: +90 212 246 1020

Ankara

Bayındır Medical Centre
Eskişehir Yolu
Sögütözü
t: +90 312 287 9000

City
Buklum Sokak, 72
Near Tunalı Hilmi Caddesi
t: +90 312 466 3366

Airlines

Turkish Airlines

Reservations
t: 663 6363
f: 240 2984

İstanbul

Aksaray
Mustafa Kemal Paşa Caddesi, 27
t: +90 212 518 6840

Harbiye
Cumhuriyet Caddesi, 199-201 (near Hilton Hotel)
t: +90 212 225 0556

A1

Sirkeci
Hamidiye Caddesi, Doğubank İşhani, 26
t: +90 212 511 7170

Taksim Square
Cumhuriyet Caddesi (near McDonalds)
t: +90 212 252 1106

Ankara

Atatürk Bulvari 125 and 231-3
Information: +90 312 419 2825;
Reservations: +90 312 419 2800
f: +90 312 418 9453

İzmir

Büyük Efes Hotel
Gaziosmanpaşa Bulvari
t: +90 232 425 8280 **f:** +90 232 483 6281

Adana

Stadyum Caddesi, 32
t: +90 322 457 0222 **f:** +90 322 454 3088

Antakya

Ant-tur Antakya Turizm ve Seyahat Acentası
İnönü Caddesi, 150
t: 214 9497 **f:** 214 2712

Bursa
Hasim Iscan Caddesi
Tugla Is Merkezi, 12/E
t: +90 224 221 1167 **f:** +90 224 222 1866

Antalya
Cumhuriyet Caddesi, 91
t: +90 242 243 4383 **f:** +90 242 248 4761

Samsun
Kazim Paşa Caddesi, 18
t: +90 362 435 2330 **f:** +90 362 431 8260

Trabzon
Atatürk Alani (square ñ south-west corner)
t: +90 462 321 1680

Diyarbakır
İnönü Caddesi, 8
t: +90 412 221 2314 **f:** +90 412 224 3366

Air France

İstanbul
Corner of Cumhuriyet and Tarlabasi Caddesi
Taksim
t: +90 212 237 3000

Ankara
Atatürk Bulvari 231/7
Kavaklıdere
t: +90 312 467 4400

Alitalia

İstanbul
Cumhuriyet Caddesi, 12/4
Elmadag
t: +90 212 231 3391

Ankara
Emek Ishani, 11th floor
Kizilay
t: 425 3813

American Airlines

Cumhuriyet Caddesi, 47/2
Elmadag
İstanbul
t: +90 212 237 2003

A1

British Airways

İstanbul
Cumhuriyet Caddesi, 10
Elmadag
t: +90 212 234 1300

Ankara
Atatürk Bulvari 237/29
Kavaklıdere
t: +90 312 467 5557

Delta Airlines
İstanbul Hilton Arcade
t: +90 212 231 2339

El Al
Rumeli Caddesi 4/1
Nişantaşı
İstanbul
t: +90 212 246 5303

Finnair and Gulf Air
Cumhuriyet Caddesi, 26
Elmadag
İstanbul
t: +90 212 234 5130

Iberia
Topcu Caddesi 2/2
Elmadag
İstanbul
t: +90 212 237 3104

İstanbul Airlines
Cumhuriyet Caddesi, 289
Elmadag
İstanbul
t: +90 212 231 7526 **f:** +90 212 246 4967

Japan Airlines
Cumhuriyet Caddesi, 141/6
Elmadag
İstanbul
t: +90 212 241 7266

KLM

İstanbul

Abdi İpekçi Caddesi, 8
Nişantaşı
t: +90 212 230 0311

Ankara

Atatürk Bulvari 127, 3rd floor
Bakanliklar
t: +90 312 417 5617

Lufthansa

Maya Akar Centre
Büyükdere Caddesi
Esentepe
İstanbul
t: +90 212 288 1050

Olympic Airlines

Cumhuriyet Caddesi, 203
Elmadağ
İstanbul
t: +90 212 246 5081

Qantas Airways

Cumhuriyet Caddesi, 155/1
Elmadağ
İstanbul
t: +90 212 240 5032

Sabena

İstanbul

Topcu Caddesi 2/1
Taksim
t: +90 212 254 7254

Ankara

Tunali Hilmi Caddesi 112/1
Kavaklıdere
t: +90 312 467 2535

SAS

Cumhuriyet Caddesi, 26/A
Elmadağ
İstanbul
t: +90 212 246 6075

A1

Singapore Airlines

Harbiye
Halaskargazi Caddesi, 113
t: 232 3706

Ankara
Tunalı Hilmi Caddesi
Bulten Sokak 17/3
Kavaklıdere
t: +90 312 468 4670

Swissair

İstanbul
Cumhuriyet Caddesi, 6
Elmadağ
t: +90 212 231 2850

Ankara
Cinnah Caddesi,1/2A
Kavaklıdere
t: +90 312 468 1144

TWA

Cumhuriyet Caddesi, 193
Elmadağ
İstanbul
t: +90 212 234 5327

Airports

İstanbul Atatürk Airport

Air France	t: +90 212 663 0600
Alitalia	t: +90 212 663 0577
British Airways	t: +90 212 663 0574
Delta Airlines	t: +90 212 663 0752
El Al	t: +90 212 663 0810
Iberia	t: +90 212 663 0826
İstanbul Airlines:	
International	t: +90 212 663 0664
Domestic	t: +90 212 574 4271
KLM	t: +90 212 663 0603
Lufthansa	t: +90 212 663 0594
Olympic Airways	t: +90 212 663 0820
Sabena	t: +90 212 663 0824
SAS	t: +90 212 663 0818
Singapore Airlines	t: +90 212 663 0710
Swissair	t: +90 212 663 6778

Ankara Esenboğa **t:** +90 212 398 0000
Izmir Adnan Menderes **t:** +90 212 274 2626

Automobile rentals

Avis

İstanbul

Central Reservations **t:** +90 212 257 2670
f: +90 212 263 3918
Atatürk Airport International Arrival **t:** +90 212 663 0646
Domestic Arrivals **t:** +90 212 573 1452
İstanbul Hilton Arcade **t:** +90 212 241 7896
Beyazit office **t:** +90 212 516 6109

Ankara

t: +90 312 467 2313

İzmir

t: +90 232 441 4417
Izmir Hilton **t:** +90 232 441 6016

Adnan Menderes Airport

t: 274 2172

Budget

İstanbul

Central Reservations **t:** +90 212 253 9200
Atatürk Airport International Arrivals **t:** +90 212 663 0858

Ankara

t: +90 312 417 5952

Izmir

t: +90 232 482 0505

Adnan Menderes Airport

t: +90 232 274 2203

Europcar

İstanbul

Atatürk Airport International Arrivals **t:** +90 212 663 0746
Taksim Square **t:** +90 212 254 7799

Ankara

t: +90 312 418 3430

İzmir

t: +90 232 441 5141

A1

Hertz

İstanbul

Atatürk Airport International Arrivals **t:** +90 212 573 5987
Opposite Hilton Hotel **t:** +90 212 234 4300

Ankara

t: +90 312 418 8440

Izmir

t: +90 232 274 2248

Sun Rent-a-Car

Taksim Square, İstanbul **t:** +90 212 246 0815

Thrifty

Ankara **t:** +90 312 436 0505

Banks

ABN-Amro
İnönü Caddesi, 15
Taksim
İstanbul
t: +90 212 293 8802 **f:** +90 212 249 2008

Adabank
Büyükdere Caddesi, 40
Meçidiyeköy
İstanbul
t: +90 212 272 6420 **f:** +90 212 272 6446

Akbank
Sabancı Centre
Levent
İstanbul
t: +90 212 270 2666 **f:** +90 212 269 7383

Alternatif
İnönü Caddesi, 76-78
Taksim
İstanbul
t: +90 212 252 6920 **f:** +90 212 252 2307

Arap Türk
Valıkonağı Caddesi,10
Nişantaşı
İstanbul
t: +90 212 225 0500 **f:** +90 212 225 0526

Avrupa Türk Yatırım
Yapı Kredi Plaza, C blok, Kat 15
Levent İstanbul
t: +90 212 279 7070 **f:** +90 212 282 6301

Banca Di Roma
Tünel Caddesi, 18
Karaköy
İstanbul
t: +90 212 251 0917 **f:** +90 212 249 6289

Bank Ekspres
Kore Şehitleri Caddesi, 43
Zincirlikuyu
İstanbul
t: +90 212 288 3838 **f:** +90 212 288 3867

Bank Mellat
Büyükdere Caddesi
Binbirçiçek Sokak, 1
Levent, İstanbul
t: 269 5820 **f:** 264 2895

Birlesik Türk Korfez
Büyükdere Caddesi, 42
Mecidiyekoy, İstanbul
t: +90 212 288 2000 **f:** +90 212 288 1217

Birlesik Yatırım
Cumhuriyet Caddesi, 16/3
Elmadağ
İstanbul
t: 231 6666 **f:** +90 212 232 1866

BNP-AK Dresdner
Taki Zafer Caddesi
Vakif Is Hani
Taksim
İstanbul
t: +90 212 293 8780 **f:** +90 212 243 6742

A1

Chase Manhattan
Yıldız Posta Caddesi, 52, Kat 11
Esentepe
İstanbul
t: +90 212 275 1280 **f:** +90 212 275 9932

Chemical
Abdi İpekçi Caddesi, 63
Maçka
İstanbul
t: +90 212 231 4010 **f:** +90 212 248 3791

Citibank
Büyükdere Caddesi, 100
Esentepe
İstanbul
t: +90 212 288 7700 **f:** +90 212 288 7760

Credit Lyonnaais
Setüstü Haktan İşhani 45/4
Kabatas
İstanbul
t: +90 212 251 6300 **f:** +90 212 251 7724

Demirbank
Büyükdere Caddesi, 122
Esentepe
İstanbul
t: +90 212 275 1900 **f:** +90 212 267 4794

Derbank
Abide-i Hürriyet Caddesi, 125
Şişli
İstanbul
t: +90 212 224 9494 **f:** +90 212 231 4759

Development Bank of Türkey
Kızılay
Ankara
t: +90 312 417 9200 **f:** +90 312 418 3967

Disbank
Yıldız Posta Caddesi, 54
Gayrettepe
İstanbul
t: +90 212 274 4280 **f:** +90 212 272 5278

Egebank
Büyükdere Caddesi, 106
Esentepe
İstanbul
t: +90 212 288 7400 ***f:*** +90 212 288 7316

Esbank
Meşrutiyet Caddesi, 141
Tepebaşı
İstanbul
t: +90 212 251 7270 ***f:*** +90 212 243 2396

Etibank
Tunus Caddesi, 33
Kavaklıdere
Ankara
t: +90 312 417 6230 ***f:*** +90 312 418 2938

Finansbank
Büyükdere Caddesi, 123
Gayrettepe
İstanbul
t: +90 212 275 2450 ***f:*** +90 212 275 2496

Garanti
Büyükdere Caddesi, 63
Maslak, İstanbul
t: +90 212 285 4040

Habib
Abide-i Hürriyet Caddesi
Gecit Sokak, 12
Şişli
İstanbul
t: +90 212 246 0220 ***f:*** +90 212 234 0807

HSBC
Cumhuriyet Caddesi, 8
Elmadağ
İstanbul
t: +90 212 231 5560 ***f:*** +90 212 230 54300

İktisat
Büyükdere Caddesi, 165
Esentepe
İstanbul
t: +90 212 274 1111 ***f:*** +90 212 274 7028

A1

İller
Atatürk Bulvari, 21
Opera, Ankara
t: +90 312 311 2672 ***f:*** +90 312 310 7459

İnterbank
Büyükdere Caddesi, 108/C
Esentepe
İstanbul
t: +90 212 274 2000 ***f:*** +90 212 272 1622

Kapital
Yapı Kredi Plaza, C blok, Kat 14
Levent
İstanbul
t: +90 212 279 7311 ***f:*** +90 212 282 6301

Kentbank
Tevfik Erdonmez Sokak, 18
Esentepe
İstanbul
t: +90 212 274 3091 ***f:*** +90 212 274 8920

Kıbrıs Kredi
Büyükdere Caddesi, 118
Zincirlikuyu
İstanbul
t: +90 212 274 4788 ***f:*** +90 212 274 6059

Koçbank
Barbaros Bulvari, Morbasari Sokak
Koza İş Merkezi, C blok
Beşiktaş
İstanbul
t: +90 212 274 7777 ***f:*** +90 212 267 2987

Osmanlı
Voyvoda Caddesi, 35-37
Karaköy
İstanbul
t: +90 212 252 3000 ***f:*** +90 212 244 6571

Pamukbank
Büyükdere Caddesi, 82
Gayrettepe
İstanbul
t: +90 212 275 2424 ***f:*** +90 212 266 6224

Parkbank
Büyükdere Caddesi
Meseli Sokak, 9
Levent
İstanbul
t: +90 212 281 4820 ***f:*** +90 212 278 0445

Saudi American
Cumhuriyet Caddesi, 233
Harbiye
İstanbul
t: +90 212 230 0284 ***f:*** +90 212 233 0201

Şekerbank
Atatürk Bulvari, 171
Kavaklıdere
Ankara
t: +90 312 417 9120 ***f:*** +90 312 425 4919

Sinai Yatırım ve Kredi
Akdogan Sokak 41-43
Beşiktaş
İstanbul
t: +90 212 259 7414 ***f:*** +90 212 258 7154

Société Génerale
Yapı Kredi Plaza, B blok, Kat 12
Levent
İstanbul
t: +90 212 279 7051 ***f:*** +90 212 282 6988

Tatbank
Kemeraltı Caddesi, 24, Kat 2-3
Karaköy
İstanbul
t: +90 212 249 5040 ***f:*** +90 212 249 4685

A1

Tekfenbank
Büyükdere Caddesi, 103/7
Meçidiyeköy
İstanbul
t: +90 212 275 2013 **f:** +90 212 272 8356

Tekstilbank
Abide-i Hürriyet Caddesi
Gecit Sokak,10
Şişli
İstanbul
t: +90 212 224 1313 **f:** +90 212 232 8313

Toprakbank
Büyükdere Caddesi
Nilufer Han, 103/1
Meçidiyeköy
İstanbul
t: +90 212 288 4120 **f:** +90 212 272 5619

Türk Bostan
Yıldız Posta Caddesi, 17
Esentepe
İstanbul
t: +90 212 274 5222 **f:** +90 212 272 3348

Türk Ekonomi
Meclis-i Mebusan Caddesi, 35
Fındıklı
İstanbul
t: +90 212 251 2121 **f:** +90 212 249 6568

Türk Merchant
Cevdet Paşa Caddesi, 288
Bebek
İstanbul
t: 257 7684 **f:** 257 7327

Türk Sakura
Büyükdere Caddesi, 108/A
Esentepe
İstanbul
t: +90 212 275 2930 **f:** +90 212 272 4270

Türk Ticaret
Yıldız Posta Caddesi, 2
Gayrettepe
İstanbul
t: +90 212 288 5900 **f:** +90 212 288 6113

Türkish
Valı Konagı Caddesi, 7
Nişantaşı
İstanbul
t: +90 212 225 0330 **f:** +90 212 225 0353

Türkiye Emlak
Büyükdere Caddesi, 43
Maslak
İstanbul
t: +90 212 276 1620 **f:** +90 212 276 1659

Türkiye İhracat Kredi
Milli Mudafaa Caddesi,20
Bakanlıklar
Ankara
t: +90 312 417 1300 **f:** +90 312 425 7896

Türkiye İmar
Büyükdere Caddesi, 42-46
Meçidiyeköy
İstanbul
t: +90 212 275 1190 **f:** +90 212 266 5514

Türkiye İş
Atatürk Bulvari, 191
Kavaklıdere
Ankara
t: +90 312 428 1140 **f:** +90 312 425 0750

Türkiye Kalkinma
Necatibey Caddesi, 98
Bakanliklar
Ankara
t: +90 312 231 8400 **f:** +90 312 231 3125

Türkiye Sinai Kalkınma
Meclis-i Mebusan Caddesi, 137
Fındıklı
İstanbul
t: +90 212 251 2800 **f:** +90 212 243 2975

Tütünbank
Barbaros Bulvari, 121
Balmumcu
İstanbul
t: +90 212 275 8400 **f:** +90 212 272 8314

Westdeutsche Landesbank
Nisbetiye Caddesi, 38, Kat 1-2
Levent
İstanbul
t: +90 212 279 2537 **f:** +90 212 280 2941

Yapı ve Kredi
Büyükdere Caddesi
Yapı Kredi Plaza, A blok
Levent
İstanbul
t: +90 212 280 1111 **f:** +90 212 280 1670

Yatırım
Dr Sevket Bey Sokak, 5
Şişli
İstanbul
t: +90 212 225 7090 **f:** +90 212 231 9599

Yürtbank
Cumhuriyet Caddesi, 16, Kat 5-6
Elmadağ
İstanbul
t: +90 212 225 8779 **f:** +90 212 224 5861

Chambers of commerce

Union of Chambers of Commerce, Industry, Maritime Commerce and Commodity Exchanges of Türkey
Atatürk Bulvari, 149
06640 Bakanlıklar
Ankara
t: +90 312 418 3360 **f:** +90 312 418 3268

İstanbul Chamber of Commerce
Ragıp Gumuspala Caddesi, 84
34378 Emınönü
İstanbul
t: +90 212 511 4150 **f:** +90 212 526 2197
Website: [www.tr-ito.com]

İstanbul Chamber of Industry
Meşrutiyet Caddesi, 118
80050 Tepebaşı
İstanbul
t: +90 212 252 2900 **f:** +90 212 249 3963

Chamber of Maritime Commerce
Meclisi Mabusan Caddesi, 22
80154 Salı Pazarı
İstanbul
t: +90 212 252 0130 **f:** +90 212 293 7935

Ankara Chamber of Commerce
Eskisehir Yolu
Söğütözü
Ankara
t: +90 312 286 4036 **f:** +90 312 286 3446

Ankara Chamber of Industry
Atatürk Bulvari, 193/4
Kavaklıdere, Ankara
t: +90 312 417 1200 **f:** +90 312 417 2060

İzmir Chamber of Commerce
Atatürk Caddesi, 126
35210 Paşaport
t: +90 232 441 7777 **f:** +90 232 483 7853

Adana Chamber of Commerce
Seyhan Caddesi, 67
t: +90 322 359 7872

Embassies

UK

Şehit Ersan Caddesi 46/A
Çankaya
t: 468 6230 **f:** 468 3214
E-mail: [britembank@superonline.com]

A1

US
Atatürk Bulvari, 110
Kavaklıdere
t: 468 6110 **f:** 467 0019
Website: [www.usis-ankara.org.tr/main.htm]

Australia
Nene Hatun Caddesi, 83
06700 Gaziosmanpaşa
t: 446 1180 **f:** 446 1188

Canada
Nene Hatun Caddesi, 75
06700 Gaziosmanpaşa
t: 436 1275 **f:** 446 4437

New Zealand
Level 4, Iran Caddesi, 13
Kavaklıdere
t: 467 9054 **f:** 467 9013
E-mail: [newzealand@superonline.com.tr]

Consulates in İstanbul

UK
Meşrutiyet Caddesi, 34
Tepebaşı
t: 293 7545 **f:** 245 4989
E-mail: brcgist@verisoft.com.tr

US
Meşrutiyet Caddesi, 104-108
Tepebaşı
t: 251 3602 **f:** 267 0057

Australia
Tepecik Yolu, 58
80630 Etiler
t: 257 7050 **f:** 257 7054

Canada
Büyükdere Caddesi, 107/3
Bengun Han, 3rd Floor
Gayrettepe
t: 272 5174

New Zealand
Maya Akar Centre, 24th Floor
Büyükdere Caddesi, 100-102
Esentepe
t: 275 2989 **f:** 275 5008

A1

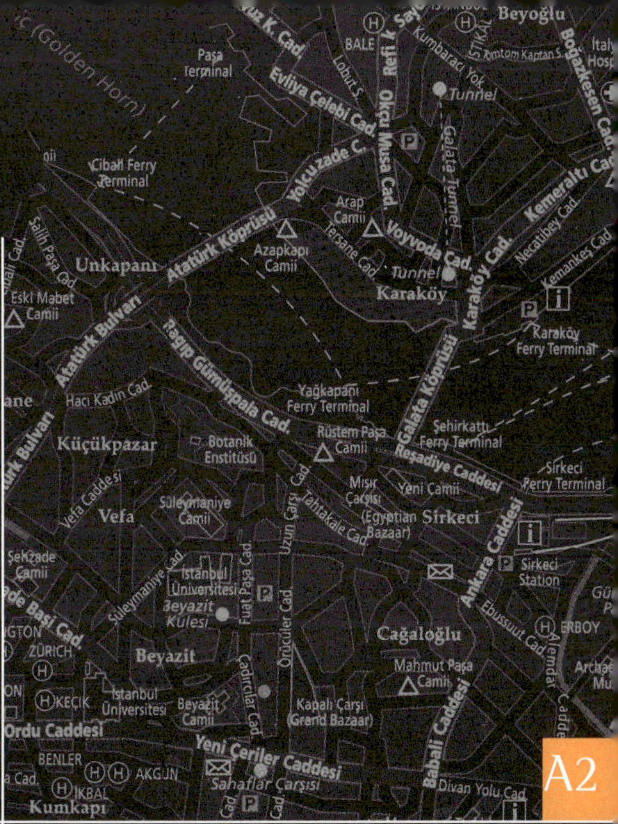

A2

appendix two

appendix two

A2

Turkish Lanugage

Turkish is the most widely spoken language in the Turkic group of languages, which are spoken across the Caucasus, Central Asia and parts of China. Turkish is a very ancient language and Turks are justifiably proud of their language and literary tradition. Making fun of the language can land you in trouble.

Atatürk's reforms included abandoning the Arabic script for the language and the adoption of a modified version of the Latin script. Once you have learnt the modifications, this makes reading and pronouncing Turkish relatively simply. There are also other features that make Turkish an attractive language – it is one of the most regular in the world with only one irregular verb and noun and uses a system of vowel agreement, which helps with predicting the spelling of a word. However, its practice of agglutination (adding prefixes and suffixes to a root) and unfamiliar word order can make it a difficult language to master with any fluency.

Pronunciation

Almost all words in Turkish are pronounced as they are spelt, with each letter pronounced separately. Letters do not combine to produce a different sound as 's' and 'h' do in English. The only exception to this is the letter ğ which is silent and lengthens the vowel in front of it, so 'a' become 'ah'.

The letters that are not pronounced as in English are:

ı (undotted i) a short 'u' sound as in 'bus'
ö as the word 'oh'
ü as the word 'yew'
c as 'j' in 'jet'
ç as 'ch' in 'church'
g is always a hard 'g' as 'goat'
h is always pronounced
j as 's' in 'measure'
ş as 'sh' in 'English'

The letter 'w' only appears in words borrowed from foreign languages and is pronounced as 'v'.

A2

Basic Phrases

Greetings and common expressions

Hello	Merhaba
Good morning/ Good day	Gunaydın
Good evening	İyi akşamlar
Good night	İyi geceler
Goodbye (said by the person leaving)	Allaha ısmarladık
Goodbye (said by the person staying)	Gule gule
Bon Apptite	Afiyet olsun
Your health	Şerefinize
How are you?	Nasılsınız?
Very well	Çok iyiyim
Yes	Evet
No	Hayır
Please	Lütfen
Thank you	Teşekkur ederim
Thanks (less formal)	Teşekkurler
You're welcome	Bir şey değil
Pardon me	Affedersiniz
Help yourself	Buyurunuz
What?	Ne?
How?	Nasıl?

Who?	Kim?
Why?	Niçin neden?
When?	Ne zaman?
Which one?	Hangisi
What's this?	Bu ne?
Where is ...?	Nerede?
How much?	Kac?
Hot	sıcak
Cold	soğuk
Big	büyük
Small	kücük
Open	açık
Closed	kapalı
Good	iyi
Bad	fenah
Beautiful	güzel

Locations

Airport	hava lımanı
Bus station	otogar
Street (main)	Caddesi
Street (side)	Sokak
Boulevard	Bulvari
Square	Meydan

Embassy	Büyükelçiliği
British embassy	Ingiliz Büyükelçiliği
Consulate-general	Başkonsolosluğu
Bureau de change	kambiyo
Post office	postane
Working hours	çalışma saatleri
Hospital	hastane
Hotel	otel

A2

Directions

Left	sol
Right	sağ
Here	burada
Near	yakın
Far	uzuk

Numbers

0	sıfır	20	yirmi
1	bir	30	otuz
2	iki	40	kırk
3	üç	50	elli
4	dört	60	altmış
5	beş	70	yetmiş
6	altı	80	seksen
7	yedi	90	doksan
8	sekiz	100	yüz
9	dokuz	200	iki yüz
10	on	1000	bin
11	on bir	2000	iki bin
12	on iki	10000	on bin
13	on üç	1000000	milyon

1/2(when used on own) yarım
1/2 (when used with whole number) buçuk
e.g. 11/2 bir buçuk

Time

Today	bugün
Tomorrow	yarın
Yesterday	dun
Sunday	Pazar
Monday	Pazartesi
Tuesday	Salı
Wednesday	Çarşamba
Thursday	Perşembe
Friday	Cuma
Saturday	Cumartesi

A2

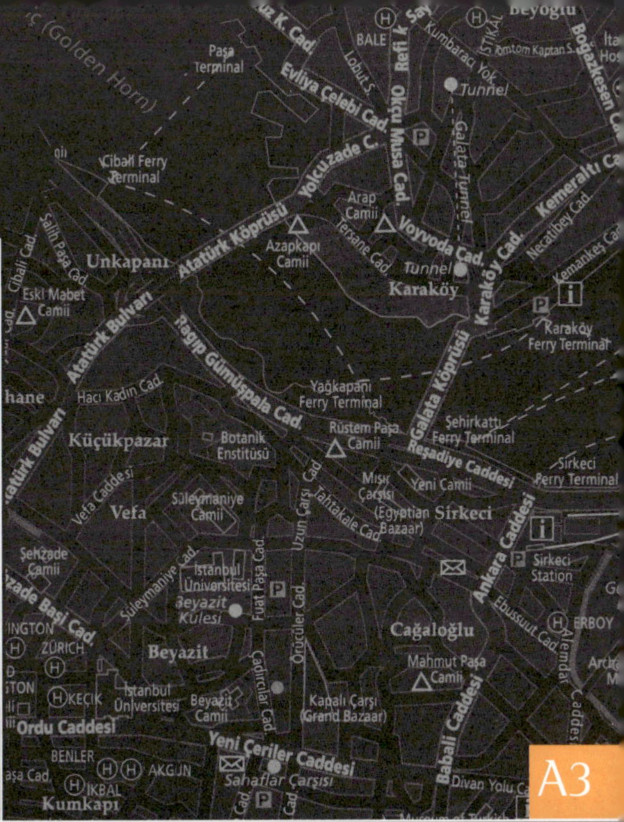

A3

appendix three

appendix three

A3

Directory of Export Assistance Centres

Cities in capital letters are centres which combine the export promotion and trade finance service of the Department of Commerce, the Export-Import Bank, the Small Business Administration and the Agency of International Development.

ALABAMA
Birmingham, Alabama - George Norton, Director
950 22nd Street North, Room 707, ZIP 35203
t: : (205) 731-1331 ***f:*** (205) 731-0076

ALASKA
Anchorage, Alaska - Charles Becker, Director
550 West 7th Ave., Suite 1770, ZIP: 99501
t: (907) 271-6237 ***f:*** (907) 271-6242

ARIZONA
Phoenix, Arizona - Frank Woods, Director
2901 N. Central Ave., Suite 970, ZIP 85012
t: (602) 640-2513 ***f:*** (602) 640-2518

CALIFORNIA - LONG BEACH
Joseph F Sachs, Director
Mary Delmege, CS Director
One World Trade Center, Ste. 1670, ZIP: 90831
t: (562) 980-4550 ***f:*** (562) 980-4561

CALIFORNIA - SAN JOSE
101 Park Center Plaza, Ste. 1001, ZIP: 95113
t: (408) 271-7300 ***f:*** (408) 271-7307

COLORADO - DENVER
Nancy Charles-Parker, Director
1625 Broadway, Suite 680, ZIP: 80202
t: (303) 844-6623 ***f:*** (303) 844-5651

A3

CONNECTICUT
Middletown, Connecticut - Carl Jacobsen, Director
213 Court Street, Suite 903 ZIP: 06457-3346
t: (860) 638-6950 *f:* (860) 638-6970

DELAWARE
Served by the Philadelphia, Pennsylvania U.S. Export Assistance Center

FLORIDA - MIAMI
John McCartney, Director
P.O. Box 590570, ZIP: 33159
5600 Northwest 36th St., Ste. 617, ZIP: 33166
t: (305) 526-7425 *f:* (305) 526-7434

GEORGIA - ATLANTA
Samuel Troy, Director
285 Peachtree Center Avenue, NE, Suite 200
ZIP: 30303-1229
t: (404) 657-1900 *f:* (404) 657-1970

A3

HAWAII
Honolulu, Hawaii - Greg Wong, Manager
1001 Bishop St.; Pacific Tower; Suite 1140
ZIP: 96813
t: (808) 522-8040 *f:* (808) 522-8045

IDAHO
Boise, Idaho - James Hellwig, Manager
700 West State Street, 2nd Floor, ZIP: 83720
t: (208) 334-3857 *f:* (208) 334-2783

ILLINOIS - CHICAGO
Mary Joyce, Director
55 West Monroe Street, Suite 2440, ZIP: 60603
t: (312) 353-8045 *f:* (312) 353-8120

INDIANA
Indianapolis, Indiana - Dan Swart, Manager
11405 N. Pennsylvania Street, Suite 106
Carmel, IN, ZIP: 46032
t: (317) 582-2300 ***f:*** (317) 582-2301

IOWA
Des Moines, Iowa - Allen Patch, Director
601 Locust Street, Suite 100, ZIP: 50309-3739
t: (515) 288-8614 ***f:*** (515) 288-1437

KANSAS
Wichita, Kansas - George D. Lavid, Manager
209 East William, Suite 300, ZIP: 67202-4001
t: (316) 269-6160 ***f:*** (316) 269-6111

KENTUCKY
Louisville, Kentucky - John Autin, Director
601 W. Broadway, Room 634B , ZIP: 40202
t: (502) 582-5066 ***f:*** (502) 582-6573

LOUISIANA - DELTA
Patricia Holt, Acting Director
365 Canal Street, Suite 1170
New Orleans ZIP: 70130
t: (504) 589-6546 ***f:*** (504) 589-2337

MAINE
Portland, Maine - Jeffrey Porter, Manager
c/o Maine International Trade Center
511 Congress Street, ZIP: 04101
t: (207) 541-7400 ***f:*** (207) 541-7420

MARYLAND - BALTIMORE
Michael Keaveny, Director
World Trade Center, Suite 2432
401 East Pratt Street, ZIP: 21202
t: (410) 962-4539 ***f:*** (410) 962-4529

A3

MASSACHUSETTS - BOSTON
Frank J. O'Connor, Director
164 Northern Avenue
World Trade Center, Suite 307, ZIP: 02210
t: (617) 424-5990 *f:* (617) 424-5992

MICHIGAN - DETROIT
Neil Hesse, Director
211 W. Fort Street, Suite 2220, ZIP: 48226
t: (313) 226-3650 *f:* (313) 226-3657

MINNESOTA - MINNEAPOLIS
Ronald E. Kramer, Director
45 South 7th St., Suite 2240, ZIP: 55402
t: (612) 348-1638 *f:* (612) 348-1650

MISSISSIPPI
Mississippi - Harrison Ford, Manager
704 East Main St., Raymond, MS, ZIP: 39154
t: (601) 857-0128 *f:* (601) 857-0026

MISSOURI - ST LOUIS
Randall J. LaBounty, Director
8182 Maryland Avenue, Suite 303, ZIP: 63105
t: (314) 425-3302 *f:* (314) 425-3381

MONTANA
Missoula, Montana - Mark Peters, Manager
c/o Montana World Trade Center
Gallagher Business Bldg., Suite 257, ZIP: 59812
t: (406) 243-2098 *f:* (406) 243-5259

NEBRASKA
Omaha, Nebraska - Meredith Bond, Manager
11135 "O" Street, ZIP: 68137
t: (402) 221-3664 *f:* (402) 221-3668

NEVADA
Reno, Nevada - Jere Dabbs, Manager
1755 East Plumb Lane, Suite 152, ZIP: 89502
t: (702) 784-5203 ***f:*** (702) 784-5343

NEW HAMPSHIRE
Portsmouth, New Hampshire - Susan Berry, Manager
17 New Hampshire Avenue, ZIP: 03801-2838
t: (603) 334-6074 ***f:*** (603) 334-6110

NEW JERSEY
Trenton, New Jersey - Rod Stuart, Director
3131 Princeton Pike, Bldg. #4, Suite 105, ZIP: 08648
t: (609) 989-2100 ***f:*** (609) 989-2395

NEW MEXICO
New Mexico - Sandra Necessary, Manager
c/o New Mexico Dept. of Economic Development
P.O. Box 20003, Santa Fe, ZIP: 87504-5003
FEDEX:1100 St. Francis Drive, ZIP: 87503
t: (505) 827-0350 ***f:*** (505) 827-0263

NEW YORK - NEW YORK
John Lavelle, Acting Director
6 World Trade Center, Rm. 635, ZIP: 10048
t: (212) 466-5222 ***f:*** (212) 264-1356

NORTH CAROLINA - CAROLINAS
Roger Fortner, Director
521 East Morehead Street, Suite 435, Charlotte, ZIP: 28202
t: (704) 333-4886 ***f:*** (704) 332-2681

NORTH DAKOTA
Served by the Minneapolis, Minnesota Export Assistance Center

OHIIO - CLEVELAND
Michael Miller, Director
600 Superior Avenue, East, Suite 700
ZIP: 44114
t: (216) 522-4750 *f:* (216) 522-2235

OKLAHOMA
Oklahoma City, Oklahoma - Ronald L. Wilson, Director
301 Northwest 63rd Street, Suite 330, ZIP: 73116
t: (405) 608-5302 *f:* (405) 608-4211

OREGON - PORTLAND
Scott Goddin, Director
One World Trade Center, Suite 242
121 SW Salmon Street, ZIP: 97204
t: (503) 326-3001 *f:* (503) 326-6351

A3

PENNSYLVANIA - PHILADELPHIA
Rod Stuart, Acting Director
615 Chestnut Street, Ste. 1501, ZIP: 19106
t: (215) 597-6101 *f:* (215) 597-6123

PUERTO RICO
San Juan, Puerto Rico (Hato Rey) - Vacant, Manager
525 F.D. Roosevelt Avenue, Suite 905
ZIP: 00918
t: (787) 766-5555 *f:* (787) 766-5692

RHODE ISLAND
Providence, Rhode Island - Vacant, Manager
One West Exchange Street, ZIP: 02903
t: (401) 528-5104, *f:* (401) 528-5067

SOUTH CAROLINA
Columbia, South Carolina - Ann Watts, Director
1835 Assembly Street, Suite 172, ZIP: 29201
t: (803) 765-5345 *f:* (803) 253-3614

SOUTH DAKOTA
Siouxland, South Dakota - Cinnamon King, Manager
Augustana College, 2001 S. Summit Avenue
Room SS-44, Sioux Falls, ZIP: 57197
t: (605) 330-4264 ***f:*** (605) 330-4266

TENNESSEE
Memphis, Tennessee - Ree Russell, Manager
Buckman Hall, 650 East Parkway South, Suite 348
ZIP: 38104.
t: (901) 323-1543 ***f:*** (901) 320-9128

TEXAS - DALLAS
LoRee Silloway, Director
P.O. Box 420069, ZIP: 75342-0069
2050 N. Stemmons Fwy., Suite 170, ZIP: 75207
t: (214) 767-0542 ***f:*** (214) 767-8240

UTAH
Salt Lake City, Utah - Stanley Rees, Director
324 S. State Street, Suite 221, ZIP: 84111
t: (801) 524-5116 ***f:*** (801) 524-5886

VERMONT
Montpelier, Vermont - Susan Murray, Manager
National Life Building, Drawer 20, ZIP: 05620-0501
t: (802) 828-4508 ***f:*** (802) 828-3258

VIRGINIA
Richmond, Virginia - Helen D. Lee Hwang, Manager
400 North 8th Street, Suite 540, ZIP: 23240-0026
P.O. Box 10026
t: (804) 771-2246 ***f:*** (804) 771-2390

WASHINGTON - SEATTLE
David Spann, Director
2001 6th Ave, Suite 650, ZIP: 98121
t: (206) 553-5615 ***f:*** (206) 553-7253

WEST VIRGINIA

Charleston, West Virginia - Harvey Timberlake, Director
405 Capitol Street, Suite 807, ZIP: 25301
t: (304) 347-5123 ***f:*** (304) 347-5408

WISCONSIN

Milwaukee, Wisconsin - Paul D. Churchill, Director
517 E. Wisconsin Avenue, Room 596, ZIP: 53202
t: (414) 297-3473 ***f:*** (414) 297-3470

WYOMING

Served by the Denver, Colorado U.S. Export Assistance Center

Gorilla Guides
128 Kensington Church Street, London W8 4BH
Tel: (44) 207 221 7166; Fax: (44) 207 792 9288
E-mail: enquiries@stacey-international.co.uk

business travellers'
HANDBOOKS

The series that focuses on the needs of the business traveller

The Series

- **Unique:** Nothing like this currently available in the trade market
- **Recognised:** Already widely accepted as the reference by some chambers of commerce and export desks of The Department of Trade and Industry
- **Authoritative:** Highly experienced authors with extensive business experience in the target market

The Business Travellers' Guides to

- Turkey
- Egypt
- Argentina
- The United Arab Emirates
- Saudi Arabia

Content

- **Quality and Efficiency:** Essential tips on where to stay and how to get started
- **Etiquette:** The social morés of the local business culture
- **Creating an Impression:** Where to lunch and dine a local guest; basic vocabulary and phrases
- **The nitty-gritty:** Full details of organisations offering support and advice
- **Business Overviews:** Authoritative insights into the major economic and commercial sectors
- **Contacts:** Appendixes of useful contact details